Dr. Bieler's
Natural Way
to Sexual Health

DR. BIELER'S NATURAL WAY TO SEXUAL HEALTH

Henry G. Bieler, M.D.
and
Sarah Nichols

Charles Publishing
Los Angeles

*Published in the United States by
Charles Publishing Company, Inc.,
Los Angeles, California
and simultaneously in Canada by
Copp-Clark, Toronto, Ontario*

*Library of Congress Catalog Card Number 72-83312
ISBN Number 0-912880-03-1*

First Edition November 1972

Manufactured in the United States of America

*To John Gilbert,
a humanitarian and
seeker after the truth*

ABOUT THE AUTHORS

Dr. Henry G. Bieler studied medicine at the University of Cincinnati, where he came under the lifelong influence of Dr. Martin Fischer, the great physiologist and philosopher. For over fifty-five years he has been a doctor and has treated motion picture stars, coal miners, politicians, farmers, those of the professional worlds—in fact, men and women from every walk of life. He has brought thousands of healthy babies into the world, including his own children and grandchildren. Outdoorsman, musicologist, sculptor and scientist, Dr. Bieler is his own best example of the person the patient can become. He is the author of "Food Is Your Best Medicine."

Sarah Nichols, born in Hollywood, California, was raised in Westchester County, New York.

She has taught both nutrition and exercise in Southern California health studios during her five years in the field of nutrition.

Miss Nichols and both of her sons, Roman Dana Hubbell and Soctt Hubbell, are patients of Dr. Bieler. Both Miss Nichols and her son Roman Dana have benefited, to the extent of therapeutic recoveries from serious health problems, as the result of following Dr. Bieler's personalized dietetic programs.

An Appreciation

Thanks are long overdue to my patients for the things they have taught me in more than a half century of practice.

Many thanks to Sarah Nichols for all of her contributions. I also wish to thank Alana Blumer for her helpful criticism.

To Charles Bloch who believed in my work, and to Walter R. Schmidt and Jerome Fried who helped clarify its expression, thanks also.

Foreword

Lawrence Clark Powell

Reading about the lives of the great doctors we learn that medicine as practiced by them ranges over a wide spectrum from the sciences to the arts, and even beyond to metaphysics. The healing art, medicine was once called.

That health is more than body chemistry has long been known to Dr. Henry G. Bieler. From the earliest years of his medical education at the University of Cincinnati where he came under the influence of Dr. Martin Fischer, on through his long practice of medicine in the mountain towns of his native Idaho and the coal-mining communities of Kentucky and West Virginia, then through the middle years in Pasadena, and finally to where he now lives and practices on the sea-cliff at Capistrano Beach in Southern California, this knowledge has persisted.

For over half a century Dr. Bieler has prescribed for the whole needs of man, not alone for his body. By the example of his own multifarious life as a kind of Renaissance man, the beauty of the setting in which he receives patients, and the extramedical counsel he gives them, this physician has not only made people well, he has changed their lives for good. When I first consulted him at the end of the 1920s, I had just graduated from college, exhausted from the frantic pace. After prescribing a simple dietary regimen which eliminated hamburgers, Cokes, pie, and chocolate malts, those staples of my generation, Dr. Bieler went further to help settle my roiled emotional sediment. "Try this," he said as I left his office, handling me a copy of *The Rainbow* by D.H. Lawrence.

That friendly act changed my whole literary bent and led to reading, studying, and writing about modern authors, American and European, and to my lifelong career as librarian, teacher, and writer. We have been friends through all these years, sharing interests in literature, art, music, and travel. My unbroken good health I owe to him. His faith and encouragement were limitless.

Dr. Bieler is a cellist, pianist, and singer. I recall a concert that included Brahms' *German Requiem*, in which he sang a baritone part in the chorus. He plays Bach for the joy of it. He is a sensitive accompanist.

When Dr. Bieler made his first trip to Europe during my postgraduate years in France, I served as his guide and interpreter in Paris. Music, art, and architecture filled our days and nights. His interests were wide and insatiable, his energy enormous. We examined every piece of sculpture in the Rodin Museum, where I distracted a guard while Dr. Bieler photographed one of his favorite pieces. In the Balzac, Louvre, and Luxembourg museums, we left no room unexplored. We saw the Church of Ste. Clotilde where César Franck had been organist. We climbed to the top of Notre Dame and looked down on Paris. We heard the Lener Quartet play Debussy and Ravel, and afterward on the *terrasse* of the Café de la Paix we watched high, horse-drawn vegetable carts on their way to Les Halles. Up early while I slept, he walked for miles through the wakening streets, then returned to rouse me for breakfast. At a café in Montparnasse that served certified milk, scrambled eggs, and toast, I coached him to ask for *du lait Friga, des oeufs brouillées, et du pain grillé*.

In Paris Dr. Bieler's interests took in the museum of the Faculty of Medicine on the Boulevard St. Germain, where he discoursed to me on the pickled specimens of classical diseases going back to the Middle Ages. When we went on to Germany, he became my guide and interpreter, as German is his second language.

Whatever Dr. Bieler does is done with concentration, intensity, and belief, and this irradiating vitality is an essential part of the therapy he offers patients. He is a dynamic example of his concept of health.

Chemistry, philosophy, aesthetics, travel, all contribute to man's well-being. Nature is also a part. In his Idaho boyhood Dr. Bieler was an ardent hunter and fisher. Now with camera he hunts brown bears and Rocky Mountain goats, then models them in clay and carves them in wood. In these later years, as he approaches his eightieth birthday, Dr. Bieler's summers are spent in the Rockies, at Aspen for music, West Glacier for solitude, wood carving, painting, and writing, and on into the Canadian Rockies. Throughout the mountains he has made friends with fellow wood carvers among the Indians and backwoodsmen.

By those they revere shall ye know them. Who are Dr. Bieler's medical saints? First of all, Hippocrates, one of the earliest and greatest of doctors. Then Sir William Osler and Dr. Harvey Cushing, whose *Practice of Medicine,* and *Life* are, respectively, two of Dr. Bieler's basic books. Finally, Dr. Martin Fischer, the great physiologist and philosopher who was his first teacher, whose Fischerisms and translation of Baltasar Gracian are at the Bieler bedside.

In each generation there are doctors of medicine who revitalize and transmit this ancient tradition of healing as an art based on science that goes back to the Greeks. Henry G. Bieler is such a doctor—traditionalist, scientist, artist, creative healer.

Contents

Part III: The Best in Foods

To the Reader

Every area concerning human sex has been intensively investigated, except the role of nutrition and how it affects a person's sex life. This book deals with the subject, and the information in it is based on fifty-five years of experience and research.

My premise is that practical medical knowledge rests, as it were, on the legs of a tripod. These three legs are the chemistry of metabolism, endocrinology, and psychology. In the following pages I show how I have used all three sciences in concert to provide my patients with knowledge and with healthier bodies, so that they may enjoy sexual fulfillment all of their lives.

I have long recognized that a person's sex life begins in the womb of the mother. How the prospective mother cares for herself nutritionally will determine her child's health and its glandular balance in adulthood. This, in turn, determines whether or not the person will enjoy a mature sex life.

Experience has taught me that impotence and frigidity are not usually just psychological, as is commonly accepted, but that a great deal of the time there is a chemical basis to both problems, resulting in organ pathology. In the male, there is inability to achieve or sustain an erection. In the female, there is lack of feeling (sexual anesthesia) in the genital area, so that it is impossible for her to achieve a climax. I have proven in countless cases that improper diet causes damage to and malfunction of the sex organs, and that prescribing an individual proper diet leads to restoration of the male's virility and the return of feeling to the female's genital area.

It has also been my observation through the years that toxic sexual secretions can cause local irritations and lesions. When the body is toxic, vicarious elimination can take place through the mucous membranes or skin in the genital areas, causing redness or lesions on the penis and infection in the vagina. After the body is cleansed of toxins with diet, the irritations and unpleasant secretions clear up, freeing man and woman to enjoy each other as nature intended.

The science of endocrinology has revealed how to classify individuals into three basic glandular types: adrenal, thyroid, and pituitary. In this book I explain how to recognize each type and discuss each type's sexual appetites and particular needs. I also give the general food requirements for each body type to the end that the individual can enjoy maximum pleasure in his or her sex life, thus proving that wholesome food is the best aphrodisiac.

One very basic question is: "What is sexual health?"

Sexual health is a state of wholeness, a state of physical and mental well-being, a state in which the person understands the sexual universe in which he or she lives and his or her relationship to this universe and his or her partner.

Let us examine the words "health" and "sex." By definition, a healthy person is one who is whole, free from disease or pain. He enjoys a normality of physical and mental functions — including sex. He is vital and sound.

Webster's New World Dictionary defines "sex," from the Latin *sexus,* to divide, as (1) either of the two divisions, male or female, into which persons, animals, or plants are divided, with reference to their reproductive functions; (2) the character of being male or female, all the attributes by which males and females are distinguished (the male/female energy polarity); (3) anything connected with sexual gratification or reproduction; the urge to unite; the act of sexual intercourse.

Sex, one might say, is the magnetic, electric pull of energy, the two opposites of male/female polarity attracting each other to unite in oneness, the source of all energy. Sex is the impulse toward oneness.

PART I:

FOOD
AND
SEXUAL HEALTH

FOOD—IT'S ROLE
IN YOUR SEX LIFE

1

Few people in this country today are sexually healthy.
Why?

Because we have flouted, mutilated, and broken all the
simple laws of Nature. Man, out of his frustration and his
conditioning and his desire for ease has created unnatural
food substitutes which offer little or no nutritional value.
And in his ignorance, he has stuffed himself with these foods,
disturbing his digestive system, punishing his liver and
kidneys, forcing other parts of the body, such as his
endocrine glands, sex glands, and finally his heart to
eliminate the accumulated toxins vicariously, eventually
causing ill health as we know it and sometimes premature
death.

Once we become toxic, we feel we cannot function
without continued unnatural stimulation. Our stomachs seem
to take control of our minds—surely of our common sense—
and dictate which toxic substance shall be next consumed. In
addition to dead foods, we find ourselves indulging in large
amounts of coffee, tea, chocolate, cigarettes; in far too many
instances alcoholic beverages and even drugs are craved.

However, we're not entirely to blame. We are influenced subjectively by the food industry and all forms of its advertising in the communications media. In her book *Consumer Beware,* Beatrice Trum Hunter asks, "What has happened to that 40-ounce container, the average human stomach?" A food industry executive, John W. Vassos of the Pet Milk Company, once viewed the human stomach as a merchandising problem. At a congressional hearing he said, "There is extreme competition for space in the human stomach!"

In other words, competition for those precious forty ounces puts the consumer in the position of being a valuable pawn, with each eager competitor trying his best to fill the stomach with as much of his own merchandise as possible. Most of this merchandise, unfortunately, is dead, foodless food.

Inner Pollution

We are concerned about environmental pollution, and rightly so, but what about inner pollution? Inner pollution is a state of toxemia, affecting the thinking of an individual and his energy level. Since sex is expressed in terms of energy (the orgasm, in fact, signifying the discharge of all excess energy), no one can have a complete orgasm while he is ill and malfunctioning from toxic substances in the body. The discriminatory sense cannot properly be used when the mind is being flooded with toxins circulating through the brain. Toxins affect the mind, the emotions, and the body.

Psychosomatic medicine has shown the relationship of unresolved emotional conflicts to physical illness. Time after time I have witnessed negative chemical changes in my patients' physical bodies as a result of the death of a loved one, the loss of a job, or the breakup of a marriage or love affair.

Many women patients have come to me complaining about sexual problems, the most common of these being frigidity and a feeling of being used as a sex machine, lack of tactile feeling in the nipples of the breast (usually one of the most sensitive areas in a normally healthy woman), difficulty in achieving orgasm, lack of feeling in the vagina, and, in many cases, a burning, acid sensation resulting from the man's seminal discharge.

In addition, there seems to be not only a general lack of knowledge about the effects of menopause on the sexual capabilities but, in most women, an underlying fear of menopause. As a consequence of such attitudes and ignorance of the subject, there is the feeling that once menopause is reached a woman's sex life dwindles rapidly. Nothing could be further from the truth. This conviction is supported by my personal observations, and further fortified by the research done by William Masters, M.D., and Virginia Johnson on the treatment of sexual dysfunction, reported in their recent book, *Human Sexual Inadequacy.*

When women are in their early forties—and older—they should look and be at their best. Usually their families have been raised; they have gained wisdom and maturity through experience; they have learned how to care for themselves, how to dress and to carry themselves, and they have much to share with their husbands. After menopause, they have sexual freedom and no longer have to worry about birth control pills and other contraceptives that interfere with full sexual enjoyment.

According to Masters and Johnson, the often expressed concept that aging women do not maintain a high level of sexual orientation has little or no basis in fact. The main difference is the slower production of vaginal lubrication by the older woman. In younger women, lubrication is naturally evident within fifteen to thirty seconds of initiation of the excitement stage of the sexual response cycle. In older women it may sometimes take four or five minutes of sexual play before any significant degree of lubrication develops.

Also the orgasmic phase of the 50-to-70-year-old woman is usually briefer than that of the younger woman. The average pattern of contractions recurs four or five times in the former, as opposed to the average pattern of eight to twelve recurrent contractions for the younger woman.

My male patients' complaints about their sex lives vary. Within different age groups they complain of impotence, premature ejaculation, and acid burns on the penis after entering into a woman. (These acid burns are caused by the toxic secretions eliminated vicariously through the woman's vagina.) Some men believe that women have become too aggressive or too frigid. Some believe that women have lost their sense of self-worth and jump in and out of too many beds.

As Masters and Johnson describe the older man's sexual potential, most do not establish erective response to effective sexual stimulation for a matter of minutes, as opposed to a matter of seconds for younger men. Also, the erection may not be as full or as demanding as that to which the older man was previously accustomed. If natural delays in reaction time are appreciated, however, there will be no panic on the part of either husband or his partner. If, however, the aging male is uninformed and not anticipating delayed physiological reactions to sexual stimuli, he may indeed panic; he may in fact try to force an erection, which can be harmful psychologically. Most men as they age should be prepared to notice either total absence or marked reduction in the amount of preejaculatory emission.

From the aspect of time span, the plateau phase usually lasts longer for the older man than for the younger. When the former attains a level of elevated sexual tension, he can usually maintain this level of enjoyment for an indefinite period without reaching a climax. One of the distinct advantages of the aging process is that control of the ejaculatory demand in the 50 to 70 age group is far better than in the 20 to 40 group. So Bernard Shaw's saying, "What a pity youth is wasted on the young!" is not always true, especially when it comes to ejaculatory control.

A Toxic Case

Sometimes a patient is so toxic, so ill from his toxemia, that his sexual responses cease entirely since there is not enough energy for intercourse. And often, when the liver and kidneys are damaged from an overload of toxic wastes, the male's prostate gland tries to help eliminate the overload. This was the case with a 60-year-old man from Los Angeles, California. His examination showed high blood pressure (200/160) and sixty pounds of toxic edema. His urine test revealed uric acid, sulfates in excess, phosphates, bile, protein poisoning, starch poisoning, sugar poisoning, and alcohol poisoning. There was no free alkalinity; he was sodium-starved. Sodium is an alkaline element necessary to maintain the acid/base equilibrium of the body. It is available in vegetables, especially in zucchini squash, string beans, and cucumbers.

This patient was a strong pituitary type who was just recovering from a coronary and had recently been divorced. He was determined to get well and to find a new partner to share his life. I have always maintained that the person who gets well and stays well is one who has an important goal in life, something he really wants to do.

I explained to my patient that the diet I was recommending to him might not be too easy to follow at first because of his ingrained habit patterns of eating, his reliance on coffee and smoking, and his overindulgence in alcoholic beverages and chocolate candies.

I prescribed grapefruit for breakfast. Lunch included rare lamb, steamed vegetables, zucchini, and string beans with a teaspoon of unsalted butter, as well as a salad of lettuce, cucumbers, and celery. At 4 o'clock he was to have a piece of fruit, a choice of pear, apple, or banana. Dinner was to be a repeat of lunch.

Four months later he had lost forty pounds, his blood pressure was down to 160/110, his urine still had some excess sulfates and bile. And he told me he had found a new female companion twenty years his junior.

On his last visit his weight had returned to normal. His blood pressure was down to 130/90. The urine test certified that he was free from toxins. He said that forming new habit patterns of eating had given him a new life. He felt he could cope with the stress, tensions, anxieties, and problems that had contributed to his heart attack; his sex drive was fulfilled.

By this cleansing of his body of toxins, through prescribing a simple diet and rest so that his liver and kidneys could repair themselves, the burden of vicarious elimination on the prostate gland was removed and he could function normally once again.

A few months after his last visit he called to tell me he had remarried. A year later I learned that he had fathered his first child, a son.

Beginning with Hippocrates, the Father of Medicine, recognition that disease results from some mismanagement of the physical environment has been considered of prime importance. Since the chief environment is chemical and centers around the food consumed by the individual, it is only natural that, when disease occurs, the finger of suspicion should point to some improper, unnatural food in the diet.

Hippocrates strongly believed that the diseased body needed a period of rest, not only physical rest but chemical rest which he considered to be more important. Chemical rest could be achieved only by eliminating the intake of dead foods, thus giving the organs of the body a chance to discharge accumulated waste products and thereby cleanse themselves. Hippocrates believed that sick bodies were impure bodies and that impure bodies discharged waste products that made the digestion of food impossible. He noted changes in the bile from normal to abnormal, a test based on careful observation.

His aphorism, "Impure bodies, the more they are nourished, the more they are hurt, for the nourishment is putrefied by vicious humors," showed the trend of his mind. Thus was born the idea that disease was a state of toxemia, and that this state of toxemia could be abolished through physical and chemical rest.

Hermann Boerhaave, one of the greatest physicians of the seventeenth century, stated that "Disease is cured with the help of Nature, which promotes a gentle resolution or a neutralization and excretion of morbific matter." He was equally strong in emphasizing that disease is an elimination process. And, just as disease is an elimination process, good health is a matter of self-education and application.

YOUR SEX LIFE
BEGINS IN THE WOMB 2

In recent years the trend has been toward natural childbirth; nothing could make me happier. In my fifty-five years of practice I have delivered thousands of children, mostly by natural childbirth including my own son and daughter. I have also delivered my own six grandchildren, who have added to my life immeasurably.

I am well into the comfortable decade of my seventies and am proud of my reward, which is the happiness in a mother's eyes when she sees her baby being born and holds the baby in her arms. This mother love has been a constant inspiration and reward as I have helped second and often third generations of mothers deliver normal, sexually healthy children.

According to geneticist Ashley Montagu, life begins not at birth but at conception. This means that a developing child is alive, not only in the sense that he is composed of living tissues, but also in the sense that from the moment of his conception he begins to react to outer stimuli, such as loud noises. In spite of his newness and his appearance, he is a living, striving human being right from the beginning. Dr.

Montagu further states that good nutrition is probably the most important single factor in the development of the child before he is born.

His mother can help him most during these earliest days by comprehending this fact: the health of her child, and the future sexual health of her child, can be better achieved with her full cooperation in matters of diet and environment.

The Lines of Defense

The human body has three lines of defense against the circulation of toxins in the blood stream. For the child developing in the womb, however, Nature has prepared not three but *five* lines of defense against these toxins.

The first line is the mother's liver, which strains out poisons from the blood that flows to the placenta, or afterbirth.

The second is the placenta itself, which tries to keep the blood pure by a chemical interchange through the smallest and finest of its blood vessels, the capillaries. The baby's blood, therefore, is really independent of the mother's. There are certain toxins, especially from putrefiable proteins in her diet, that are extremely irritating to the protective filtration membranes of the placenta. If the toxins are very strong, they can cause destruction of these membranes, leading to a disease of pregnancy called eclampsia. Damage also can be caused to the prospective mother's liver, resulting in swelling of her legs, headaches, and ultimately convulsions. If the irritated placenta is not immediately removed when convulsions occur, the mother's life is in grave danger. Labor then often starts naturally, or is induced by the physician at this point in an endeavor to save the mother's life. Frequently the doctor, if he is to save her, must perform a quick abortion to rid her of the toxic placenta, and all too often at the sacrifice of her child.

The third line of defense is the child's liver. Here, Nature is wise enough to allow all the blood coming from the mother's placenta to circulate directly through her liver by way of the umbilical cord. Even in the healthy mother and despite the protection afforded by the placenta, certain toxins nevertheless are present. The child's liver makes a great effort to strain these out, discharging the toxins into its bile. When too great an amount of toxins is present, the bile gradually turns black and fills the baby's intestines. This black bile is called meconium, and is sometimes produced in such quantities that it is ejected from the baby's bowel into the surrounding water, or amniotic fluid.

This complication never occurs in animals who exist on a natural diet. I have yet to see meconium in monkeys or other animals, unless their food has been "civilized." Nicotine, coffee, tea and chocolate, salt, sweets, starchy desserts and ice cream, alcohol, drugs (illegal or respectable, even aspirin), can all affect the proper development of the baby. So why use them? Nine months of petty sacrifice are not too much to pay for a fine child!

The fourth line of defense is the baby's kidneys. Here again it must be noted that the baby's kidneys are not supposed to function as filters or to secrete urine until after the child has been born. It is sometimes necessary for them to function during the last three months of pregnancy when the baby's liver is not able to carry the entire load of toxins acquired from its toxic mother. Urine is then excreted into the amniotic fluid (which can even *smell* of stale urine), and the child is surrounded by a much larger quantity of water than normal. This leads to an increase in the size of the abdomen of the mother and a greater dilatation of her abdominal cavity, both needlessly. What is worse, the toxins which the child's kidneys are trying to eliminate often cause damage to the baby's lungs, resulting in complications after its birth.

Finally, as a fifth line of defense, there are the child's endocrine glands. Overactivity of the adrenals, caused by the child's efforts to eliminate his mother's toxicity, induces the premature liver and kidney function described above.

The thyroid also tries to help elimination through the (outer) skin and mucous membranes (inner skin). As a result of the baby's thyroid's effort to lessen the toxic load imposed upon it before birth, the child is often so throttled after birth by mucus in its throat that it is necessary to remove the mucus before normal breathing can occur.

Birth Complications

Enforced overactivity of the thyroid can cause a nervous baby in the womb, one that is constantly kicking and turning somersaults and getting into abnormal intrauterine positions. The birth presentation of perfectly normal babies, as we know, is head first, because the head, being naturally the heaviest part, lies lowest in the womb.

There can be further danger to the baby if the mother's thyroid gland becomes enlarged and hyperactive during the pregnancy. When there is a disturbed or overactive thyroid *before* pregnancy, the ensuing hyperactivity can induce symptoms ranging from simple nervousness and insomnia to pernicious vomiting which may prove fatal to her and her unborn child.

Whereas an attempt to detoxicate the expectant mother should be considered through proper diet, accelerated skin and bowel elimination, and proper bed rest and quiet, the orthodox procedure consists of administration of sedative drugs or drugs that inhibit the thyroid. Thalidomide once headed this list. When it was ingested, all the disagreeable symptoms of early pregnancy disappeared. Its action was so miraculous that, by word of mouth, without advertising or ballyhoo, it became the favorite pacifier of pregnant mothers. But it was not long before its hideous disfiguring aftereffects were seen.

The reason for the resulting deformation of babies from its use became plain. During pregnancy, a hormone is needed to facilitate the rapid growth and multiplication of cells of the growing embryo. This hormone comes from the thyroid gland and impregnates the small white cells (lymphocytes) of the mother's blood. The umbilical cord consists of three groups of vessels: a vein, one artery and a large lymph channel. The impregnated white cells flow through the lymph channel to the placenta, which they penetrate by amoeboid movements, to circulate freely into the baby's lymphatic channels. To allow for the rapid growth and development of the fetus there are more of these cells in the growing embryo than there are in the child after it is born. Any drug (or poison) that interferes with the proper balance of the thyroid hormone (an iodine compound) will stop growth. Even when the whole embryo is not destroyed by this imbalance, parts of the body will still be defective, often with the result that extremities are defored or completely unformed at birth.

Since the Thalidomide disaster, "milder" drugs have been prescribed for the mother's comfort, but even the mildest of these, aspirin for instance, may be harmful to her kidneys as well as to the baby's. In my opinion the best prescription is to take *no* medication during pregnancy, *no* drugs of any kind.

Overuse of salt in the mother's diet is a hazard that can cause the baby to appear dry and shriveled, the "little old man" type of child which looks more prune than human at birth. Many a baby's secretions and excretions are so full of this common mineral as to cause eye irritations and inflammations of the skin and bowels.

A complication that can make for what a doctor might call a "messy" birth sometimes occurs when the sweat glands and sebaceous glands excrete into the amniotic fluid. When the sebaceous glands become overactive (a result of abnormal fats in the mother's blood), the child may be born covered with a white, smelly cheese, called scientifically *vernix caseosa,* that is often difficult to wash off. Such complications never happen to healthy animal babies.

Just as the mother's diet can be too salty, it can also be too sweet. Excess white sugar in the mother's diet during pregnancy will often cause distressing skin irritations in the baby. I have seen sugar-related eczemas that were very severe. One child had so critical an irritation that its skin resembled raw beefsteak; with the utmost medical care eight months were required to cure it.

Smokers beware! The poison from cigarettes (nicotine) is, among other deleterious factors, a thyroid gland depressant; if the mother smokes heavily during her pregnancy it may lead to nervous and mental afflictions in the child. Other nicotine-induced abnormalities may include premature birth, or abortion of the unborn child. In one study of 7,500 patients who were pregnant it was established that the incidence of abortion and premature birth was nearly twice as great for smoking mothers as for nonsmoking mothers. Also the average weight of newborn infants of mothers who smoked regularly throughout their pregnancy was 170 grams less than the weight of infants of mothers who never smoked. It is possible that nursing infants likewise are affected, traces of nicotine having been found in the milk of mothers who smoke.

The mother must be careful, too, of her drinking water, which is being adulterated with salt and with chlorine gas in many communities. When this condition exists, I suggest adding to a gallon of tap water a small handful of finely cut, fresh new grass (wheat grass is best). Shake the mixture slightly, and strain and bottle it. It will taste as sweet and pure as mountain snow water.

Morning Sickness

In the early months of pregnancy, as the estrogen level rises and the thyroid gland becomes hyperactive, the symptoms of "morning sickness" usually occur, especially if the woman's body is toxic. The bile, with its changed chemistry, becomes more irritating. From midnight to morning is the liver's greatest period of detoxication and elimination; the woman awakens with a toxic "hangover," which Nature seeks to rid her of in the easiest possible way—by vomiting. If the patient is extra toxic, this elimination continues throughout the day; there may be nausea and vomiting spells during the entire twenty-four hours. Occasionally, toxemia is so extremely high that this reaction is more or less continuous. Called the pernicious vomiting of pregnancy, this state may be serious enough to require abortion to save the prospective mother's life.

In some cases where pernicious vomiting is evident, it is best to cleanse the stomach and thus neutralize the toxic bile. This is accomplished by having the mother-to-be mix one level teaspoon of baking soda into twenty-four ounces of lukewarm water, then drink the mixture as rapidly as possible after her ablutions. This is an extremely nauseating mixture which induces vomiting, but the baking-soda solution most likely has cleansed the stomach. Occasionally a patient is not induced to vomit. The soda water nevertheless acts as a gentle laxative, and cleanses the stomach as it subsequently is eliminated through the urine.

After the soda-water emesis, it is best to refrain from food until definite hunger is felt, which might be a matter of a few hours. Then try one or two pieces of very dry bread. Oven-dried is better than toasted; no sweets or butter are allowed.

As soon as the nausea leaves, one cake of fresh yeast or one teaspoon of active dry yeast is prescribed, to be taken with a glass of hot water early in the morning and always unaccompanied by other food.

For the woman who suffers morning sickness, the noon meal consists of one kind of starch (brown rice, bread, or boiled potato), butter, one or two cooked vegetables (soft fresh squash and string beans), and plain lettuce, celery, or cucumber. There should be no fluids, except water if desired.

During the afternoon, one kind of fruit may be eaten, or just a glass of water.

At the evening meal, meat is permitted, either rare beef or lamb, or a few pecans or almonds for protein, small portions of starch, butter, and cooked and raw vegetables. Of course, no salt or MSG (monosodium glutamate) or condiments should be eaten. Fruit may be postponed until bedtime.

During the fifth month of pregnancy it is well to maintain a good calcium balance. If calcium pills are not available, calcium can be obtained by daily ingesting a piece of eggshell about half the size of a dime. This can be fragmented, or powdered, and easily swallowed with cooked vegetables.

As the pregnancy progresses into the seventh month it is best to discard meat, which may be overly toxic at this point, and instead drink one or two glasses of raw certified (never pasteurized or homogenized) milk a day, and once a week a raw egg yolk.

Diet at Birth

During the last three weeks of pregnancy, starch foods should be omitted. Raw and cooked vegetables, one or two glasses of raw milk, and fruit or fruit juice will prove most beneficial. Avoid strawberries, apricots, Thompson seedless grapes, cranberries, and cantaloupe.

As soon as labor pains commence, *take no food at all.* Water is allowed. After several hours of labor, if the patient is feeling weak a glass of warm water containing two well-rounded teaspoons of honey or raw sugar may be taken. This will increase the force of the contractions.

For twenty-four hours following delivery the mother generally will lose any appetite she may have felt for solid food; she usually feels dry and thirsty. Unsweetened pineapple, apple, or grape juice may be diluted with equal parts of water; papaya nectar (Hawaiian) is especially helpful. If the patient likes the flavor she is encouraged to drink about two quarts a day for the first two days.

The third day she is given, at noon and at suppertime, a large salad of plain (that is, without dressing) lettuce, celery, and cucumber; also cooked zucchini, string beans, and a little butter. The diluted fruit juices are continued, every two hours, between meals.

When this three-day rule is followed, such common complications as fever, breast and womb infection, milk leg (phlebitis), and embolic accidents rarely happen. During the last fifty-five years, while I have been prescribing this regime, not one of my patients has ever been bothered with such disorders. The mother's womb shrinks readily to its normal size and is not left large and boggy, as often happens when the wrong diet is used.

The three-day fast after delivery is most important. During this time animals eat *nothing,* with the possible exception of the afterbirth, which contains an extremely alkaline and beneficial hormone. The main reason for the fast is to allow the mother's liver plenty of time to dissipate the excess protein in the blood, resulting from the shrinking of the womb. The womb, which has expanded during pregnancy to about the size of a watermelon, diminishes in size to that of a pear. There must be a rearrangement of womb-muscle protein. While the liver is busy with this function, it is better not to encumber it with food.

The fourth day, milk may be added. As the mother's milk is created, the fruits and juices are discontinued and she lives on three or four glasses of raw milk a day for protein, on bread, potatoes, rice, or cereals for starches, plus copious amounts of raw and cooked vegetables and good butter. Occasionally the mother will develop catarrhs or headaches from the milk she drinks. If this occurs, rare beef or lamb, or almonds or pecans, may be substituted.

Exercise for the pregnant woman is not a must except when she is sedentary or obese. An active and healthy prospective mother gets plenty of exercise doing her usual chores. She can enjoy walking, swimming, tennis, and badminton if she is accustomed to such activities, as long as she is comfortable. If the fetus is well implanted, firmly fixed in the uterus, no exercise or accident can cause trouble.

If the mother must continue a sedentary or office job well into her pregnancy, I recommend that she follow a rule of mine (which is just as good for the nonpregnant woman): lie flat on the floor for five minutes out of every sixty. This position eases muscular tension in the back and pelvis, relaxes the tissues, and most importantly relieves the congestion in the liver, the main area of later possible troubles.

Many of my patients have asked me about sexual intercourse during pregnancy. I advise intercourse up until the seventh month. Positions should be avoided that would involve pressure on the woman's abdomen.

For psychological reasons, a continuation of sexual relations during most of the pregnancy is believed by present-day authorities to be important to both husband and wife. In fact, to deprive them of sex during the entire period of pregnancy could endanger the marriage. Gentleness, consideration, the use of lubricants, cleanliness, and avoidance of the flexed position (in which the woman's knees are drawn up almost to the breast) will reduce the physical risks to both mother and child.

The stimulation or caressing of the nipples should be avoided, particularly late in pregnancy. Such stimulation in the pregnant or nursing woman causes a marked contraction of the uterus. After a child is born, when he is nursing vigorously, this stimulation serves the useful purpose of promoting a quick return of the uterus to its normal size. Before birth, however, contractions of this kind may be harmful to the child. They may cause a decrease in the oxygen supply and result in damage to the unborn infant.

The reason for my belief that intercourse should cease by the seventh month is that parents who have union right up until childbirth may have babies covered with vernix caseosa, a substance described earlier, which can do harm to the newborn child. After the child is born, at least a month should elapse before the couple again resumes intercourse.

ABORTION AND MISCARRIAGE

3

For many years there were two terms that were hardly ever mentioned in polite society: "abortion" and "venereal disease." Both connoted shame.

When I was a freshman university student, I was disturbed by a lecture on venereal disease and its horrors. I remember that one student in the audience fainted. And it was also only recently that the word "abortion" became admitted to polite conversation.

Now, after all my years of active practice, I look back and wonder at our naivete and ignorance, until I realize that even today too many people are ill-informed on these two subjects.

There are three kinds of abortion: legal, illegal, and natural. The first two are surgical abortions, generally performed after the first missed period and no later than the second missed period so as not to endanger the mother. The third or natural kind, the miscarriage, results when Nature steps in and performs the operation.

There was a time when abortion was considered such a moral and social offense that penitentiary sentences were meted out to those committing it. At present, legal abortion is practiced in many countries, for example the Soviet Union, Japan, and Sweden, and in some states of the United States.

Fifteen states have recently liberalized their abortion laws, and legislation along similar lines is pending in several others. In three of those fifteen states—Hawaii, Alaska, and New York—a legal abortion may be obtained for any reason; the decision to have an abortion is left solely to the woman and her doctor. In Arkansas, Colorado, Delaware, South Carolina, Oregon, and Virginia the law presently allows abortions to be performed if the pregnancy endangers the physical or mental health of the mother, if the child is likely to be born deformed, or if the pregnancy resulted from rape or (except in Georgia) from incest. In California, an abortion is now legal if the pregnancy threatens the mother's health, or if it resulted from rape or incest, but not to prevent the birth of a deformed child.

In states with stringent abortion laws, illegal abortion is widely practiced. The illegal abortionist rarely gets caught. According to statistics, many thousands of illegal abortions occur yearly in the United States, yet one seldom reads of an abortionist's arrest.

A Personal Experience

Ten years ago I underwent an uncomfortable experience. Two patients of mine had a daughter who became pregnant at a student orgy. She had an illegal abortion performed at about two-and-a-half months. The afterbirth remained rather firmly attached to the womb. The abortionist had failed to remove all the afterbirth and the small remaining pieces caused a succession of hemorrhages.

While spending a weekend near my home on the West Coast, the girl suddenly began to bleed profusely. I was called. I sent her to a nearby hospital, in the meanwhile telephoning a colleague to care for her. I suspected that her body was trying to expel fragments of afterbirth through the mouth of the womb.

The attending doctor had noted in her chart the diagnosis of incomplete abortion. That afternoon I went to the hospital to see her, as a family friend, and was informed by the head nurse that two plainclothesmen were waiting to talk to me.

I was accused of having been the one who performed the abortion. The two police officers had put the patient through severe questioning, in spite of her nervous and weak condition. They had persisted in trying to get her to confess that I was the abortionist; with equal stubbornness she refused to name the real abortionist. In the end they were finally convinced of my innocence, although it would have been much less wearing if the patient had named the real one.

The Natural Abortion

The most frequent abortions of all are natural abortions, called miscarriages, so frequently brought about by assaulting the system with toxic foods.

I often have female patients come to me who are desirous of having children, but who cannot because of recurring natural abortions. That is what happened to a 29-year-old patient from the Midwest. Very toxic during pregnancy, she spotted at six months and miscarried at seven. She had had seven miscarriages, each of which had occurred when she was seven months pregnant.

I first saw her in 1967, after her seventh miscarriage. She was six-and-a-half months pregnant and had begun to spot. She looked pale and had edema of the legs and frequent intense headaches. I noticed that her hands showed a thick, indurated, red, scaly eczema. Since this condition is caused by too much sugar, I looked for additional signs of sugar poisoning. This was found in her childhood history of chronic endometritis; she had experienced chronic eczema on her hands and arms since birth. The reason for her miscarriages was thus explained.

I put her on a sugar-free diet and, as a result, she soon

stopped spotting and carried the baby to full term with normal delivery. Before she gave birth, her eczema had completely healed, and there was no sign of it being carried over to her newly-born baby son.

When a woman becomes toxic, one of the avenues of vicarious elimination is through the womb. Acrid, irritating material is flushed out in the menstrual blood, causing very disagreeable periods. The inflamed womb is left in a boggy condition, which makes implanting of the fertilized egg difficult, with the contents of the pregnant uterus often disgorged in one of the menstrual cycles. An abortion has occurred "naturally," although I consider miscarriage resulting from faulty diet to be a crime *against* Nature!

I often wonder why the great research work of the late Dr. Francis Pottenger, Jr., has been forgotten. Pottenger's work showed beyond all doubt the ill-effects of overcooked proteins on carnivorous animals. In his experiments, cats were used. In addition to developing many of the ailments so often seen in toxic humans, these cats were unable in the third generation to conceive at all.

The second-generation kittens were weak and sickly; no amount of proper diet, in this case raw meat, would restore them to health. Many of these kittens were born dead. The increasing inflammation of the wombs of the third generation of cats kept them sterile. Even their bowel movements were so toxic that weeds refused to grow in soil "fertilized" by their excreta. Unbelievably, very few doctors even refer to Pottenger's great work.

There is no reason to fear a lessening in the number of progeny because of abortions. One day, as our knowledge grows, natural abortion—or so-called miscarriage—will disappear. And as to the other abortions, motherhood and the sense of fulfillment it brings is too deeply rooted in life itself for the species ever to die out.

FOOD AND SEX HABITS BEGIN IN THE HOME

In this era of expansive change, medicine has made revolutionary advances in the relief of man's diseases. Man is now treated as a total being, his emotional health given the same consideration as his physical health.

Ancient Greek physicians recognized that any disturbance of the mind or the emotions affected the physical body. The emergence of psychosomatic medicine as a recognized specialty supports this early view. *Psychosomatic* is derived from Greek words meaning "soul" and "body."

Dr. Walter C. Alvarez, a specialist in psychosomatic medicine at the Mayo Clinic, has found that in many instances an emotional disturbance can aggravate physical illness. Physical disorders of all kinds have been found so closely linked with emotion that, in many of the leading medical centers of the country, doctors generally investigate the emotional factors before making a final diagnosis.

With the recognition that mind, emotions, and health were interlocked came an even greater discovery. Medical men found that the greatest causes of emotional illness were sex conflicts and sex frustrations. When I speak of sex, I do not mean the physical act alone; I also mean emotional security, because sex and love are intermingled. Physical sex is only the outward symbol of the need to give and receive love. Sexual frustration means love frustration; together they spell insecurity. A human being who goes through life being denied love can never feel secure. The first feelings of insecurity grow to conviction, then to despair. The sickness of the soul becomes the sickness of the body. And our chemical health is unbalanced as a result.

Attitude is all-important in understanding and correcting sex troubles. Man's moral sense has become highly civilized, often conflicting with his primitive instinct to find sexual gratification on any plane. Thus, guilt plays a tremendous role in illness resulting from sex conflicts. Exaggerated feelings of guilt in connection with what we do—or even what we think—sexually, can make us organically ill. Often it is not what we actually do sexually, but the self-inflicted guilt about what we do that makes us sick. And this sex guilt may be entirely unconscious.

We may go through half a lifetime with a deep maladjustment that is not discovered until some physical symptom or illness drives us to the doctor. In most cases, sexual and emotional maladjustments have their start far back in life, in childhood, and grow steadily worse through the years.

This is why sex education is so necessary in any plan of good living. Eventually, no system of education will be considered complete without teaching the interrelationship of mind, emotions, and body. If you are a parent, a grandparent, or a prospective parent, you can help teach your children, for education about sex and food begins in the home.

Children Are Sexual

Parents forget at times that children are sexual human beings from the moment they are born The sexual awakening in children is gradual and manifests itself in one form or another. The evidence of such sexual awakening varies at different ages.

The manifestation of developing sexual awareness is a good sign, not a bad sign, in children. It proves that the child is developing normally. When the child becomes curious and asks "embarrassing" questions, parents should be pleased about the child's curiosity. It indicates a healthy awareness. The normal child wants to know the "why" of everything. The little boy may ask why he can't watch his mother bathe or undress. The little girl will want to know where babies come from, and why she is made different from her brother. These are normal questions which any mother or father of a healthy child should anticipate.

Too many parents develop an anxiety about such early signs of sex awakening and sex curiosity. Forgetting their own childhood, they expect their children to be "good," that is, to act like sexless beings until they have attained full growth. During puberty parents regard sexual awareness and activity as normal—as if the child had sprung to life fully developed on a certain day. Before that day, some parents regard what is actually innocent, instinctive sex activity on the part of their children as dirty and evil.

It is in the early stage of a child's life that are planted the seeds of sexual problems which will manifest themselves in the boy's or girl's later life.

Wilhelm Stekel, a pioneer in the field of psychoanalysis, stated: "Our fate is decided in the first seven years of our lives. All that we learn later is but a superstructure built upon the first impressions and experiences." Parents' and guardians' ignorance about sexual matters, and attitudes they maintain that spring from superstitious beliefs—generally handed down by their parents—can contribute to a serious misunderstanding of sex on the part of their progeny. I sometimes think that the quotation echoing the Bible—"The iniquity of the fathers is visited upon the children"—aptly describes what all too often happens from one generation to the next. Parents who punish or scold their children for natural sex curiosity and investigation are causing serious, if not irreparable, damage to their offspring.

Children should never be told such fairy tales as "the stork brings babies." It is best to be honest with them, to give them a simple answer that they can understand, saving the finer education and details for when they are older.

No child is born sexually maladjusted. Sexual maladjustment is not an entity in itself but a symptom of a failure within the family relationship. A good sexual adjustment is greatly aided when the child is well-adjusted in nonsexual spheres. The good or bad sex adjustment in children is merely a symptom of their basic emotional reaction to family life and family attitude.

A well-balanced union invariably will foster a good family life and well-balanced children. The atmosphere of happiness, health, contentment, and harmony is transferred to the child in invisible waves. A bad relationship between parents is also transferred to the child in invisible waves, and is likely to cause emotional or sexual disturbances later on in life.

In everyday mother-father intimacy there are also hazards to a child's normal sexual development. Wilhelm Stekel's rule was: "In the presence of children act as you would before adults." Observance of this rule would automatically eliminate causes of childhood shocks which result from:

(1) Carelessness about privacy on the part of the parents during intercourse
(2) Carelessness about nudity before children
(3) Carelessness in leaving for the growing child's eye evidences of contraception or menstruation or pornographic pictures
(4) Parental indulgence in profanity or obscene language

If a child masturbates, a parent should not threaten that feeblemindedness or sickness will occur because of the act. The physical act of masturbation alone produces nothing in the way of harmful symptoms; the guilt suggested by the parent can cause damage. Threat or fear rarely breaks a child of a bad habit, they merely drive the child to secrecy.

Distraction is far better therapy than threat or punishment for childish sex play.

Fear of pregnancy is often instilled in their daughters by mothers who, mistakenly hoping to protect them, detail the difficult time *they* had in labor. The effect of such stories is often to cast a pall over happy sex lives as the youngster grows into adulthood.

Venereal disease is another threat used by some parents, even toward very young children. "You'll catch a bad disease if you don't stop that" is commonly a mother's admonition when she seeks to stop her youngster from participating in childish sex activities.

If the family has both mother and father, it is best for the mother to talk with the daughter and the boy to go to his father for advice on any questions concerning matters of sex.

The following are basic guidelines for parents in dealing with children in sex-related matters:

(1) The child is sexually susceptible throughout his life; neither pamper nor tyrannize, but give him his fair share of love and discipline. Spend time with him, and do not be too permissive or you may pay for it later.

(2) If harmful influences inside or outside the home have already caused some sexual maladjustment in your child, do not let the problem fester. If you don't have sufficient sex education to deal with it yourself, enlist the aid of your family doctor.

Often your doctor can help since he understands (and you might not) that evidences of sexual activity — including childish scratching or rubbing of the genitals, masturbation, or sex play with other children—may be caused by irritations in the youngster's sex organs. Such activity can be caused by too much salt in the diet as well as too much white sugar or products containing sugar.

Lack of threat—that is, accepting the masturbation as a normal function—and adjusting the child's diet will help him overcome the problem.

Foods for Young Children

I do not recommend meat nor do I give meat during the first two years of a child's life, since meat at that time can be acid-forming and irritating. Healthy children should be allowed, in most cases, whole grain cereal, raw milk, eggs, whole-grain bread, unsalted butter, raw honey, fruit juices, salads, steamed vegetables, red potatoes boiled in their jackets, fruit (bananas are especially good, and apples and raisins). Fruit also is fine for dessert or, if they become hungry, between meals. Sometimes the mother can make a homemade ice cream from blueberries, raw cream, and honey, then freeze it.

After the second year, meat—rare beef, lamb, boiled or broiled chicken—may be added to the menu in small amounts.

The younger that children are trained in proper habits of eating, the better. Food should be put in its proper perspective. Children are taught by their parents either to eat to live or, if the parents or grandparents overindulge in food, to live to eat. Food should be used only in moderation if the parents want to be sure of healthy children.

Parents are teachers first of all by example—by what they do, how they act, and what they believe. Parents who wish to see themselves through the eyes of their children might keep in mind the words of Martin H. Fischer, M.D., "The beginning of education lies in imitation—wherefore, pick someone worth imitating."

OUR WORST HABITS 5

The parent-teenager relationship as concerned with sex education is often a very special problem. Many parents are unfit to teach their teenage children about sex, having had little or no sex education themselves.

Parents should probably examine their own attitudes toward sex before passing them on to their growing children. The teenager can't be expected to adopt a normal attitude if the parents are suffering from sexual maladjustment, if they regard sex as something taboo or shameful. Unconsciously, the child will sense such sexual disorder or inharmony.

There should be no wall of silence between parent and teenager in discussing or dealing with any sexual problems that may arise. If the teenager cannot go to his parents with questions—or to seek help—where is he to go?

As I suggested in the last chapter, mothers should give sex education to their daughters; and fathers, or father substitutes, should educate their sons. The mother's first formal talk with her teenage daughter might describe in detail the origin of life. Also, the daughter should be told about menstruation before she begins to menstruate. The mother could tell her daughter that menstrual bleeding is Nature's way of preparing her to have a baby. When a baby is coming, menstruation stops. It is also Nature's way of flushing out toxic poisons through the eliminated blood.

If the young lady has been reared on clean foods, her menstrual period will last approximately three days; there usually is no cramping and the blood is a pure red color. Menstruation should be gentle; and, if the teenager's diet is clean, it will be mild in most cases. If the girl has indulged heavily in starches and white-sugar dead foods, her menstrual blood usually is bright red and stringy, and she will generally experience intense cramps. This type of period often necessitates bed rest. If the young lady is protein-poisoned, her menstrual flow is dark red to blackish red in color, with large clots. This type of period may hemorrhage after the third day and is very painful.

Words Create Attitudes

Never refer to menstruation as "the curse." A derogatory connotation may carry over into the daughter's sex life. With the teenager as with the younger child, it is best not to use the word "sickness," either, or imply that there is anything unclean about menstruation. The wrong attitude toward menstruation can mean a wrong attitude toward sex in general. If menstruation is made to seem unclean, or something to be resented, then sexual intercourse can seem so, too.

It is best for the mother not to pass on any anxiety about pregnancy to her daughter. Some mothers say, "If you should ever become pregnant, come and tell me about it." Many mothers use the old-hat phrase, "If you ever get in trouble. . . ." Such statements tend to convey a sense of trouble and fear; they may also seem to condone premarital sex relations. Teenage lovemaking should neither be condemned nor condoned. If you tell your daughter that "Nice girls don't pet" and thus make teenage lovemaking seem "bad," she may carry over the idea that all lovemaking is "bad" or "sinful."

Explain to her that abuse of sex, promiscuity for example, robs people of the good that sex can bring into their lives when it is a part of love, or love and marriage. Also, help her to understand that sex is neither a frightening mystery nor a toy to be experimented with for thrills. Teach her that it is a deep and natural instinct in all of us and needs to be treated with discretion if we are to be in good health and spirits.

Inspire your daughter's confidence and she will most likely feel free to come to you when she has a question or needs help.

A case from my files illustrates what can happen when a teenager, brainwashed by an ignorant woman, is made subconsciously frightened of sex, and is fed foods that unnaturally stimulate her sex glands. This girl matured physically very early. Her breasts were developed by the time she was 11. In the fifth grade, she was the only girl in her class with developed breasts. Therefore, as happens among children, she was teased and ridiculed. She had been raised by a grandmother and stepmother, her own mother having died when she was 5 years old.

Her grandmother was medieval in her attitudes about sex. The stepmother, who had had no sex education herself, either avoided the girl's questions or kept emphasizing that sex was evil. She also stressed that nice girls had sex only when married, and then sheerly for the pleasure of their husbands. The child began to accept that it was unnatural for the wife to enjoy the sex act.

This girl's conditioning, and her diet—which was heavy in cola drinks, white-sugar products, and fried, salty foods— caused a false sense of sexual stimulation, chiefly resulting from a salt and sugar irritation of the womb.

Not allowed to go out with boys until she was 15, on her very first date her unnaturally stimulated sex desire overcame her moral scruples. She had sexual intercourse. The second time she had sex she became pregnant. So ignorant was she about sexual matters that, even though she had had irregular periods, it was four months before she realized she was pregnant. Her family disowned her; the boy married her out of a sense of duty. The marriage ended in divorce. It took years of counseling, plus a cleansing diet which relieved her unnatural desires, before she could properly enjoy sex, and life overall.

Diet for the Teenager

Your daughter's diet is extremely important during the teenage period. The diet of far too many teenagers is heavy in salty foods, salty fried starches, soft drinks, ice cream, white-sugar products, preserved salted meats, pickles, and unnatural pollutant-creating foods. From 12 years on, she is easily impressed by and wants to be accepted among girl friends of the same age group. Without a strongly developed sense of self, which builds almost always from a healthy family life, she may be tempted to experiment in areas, and with peers, which could prove deleterious. For instance, she may turn to cigarettes or pot; or, if the wrong friends she chooses drink alcoholic beverages, she may try drinking also.

My files are filled with case histories of teenage girls with menstrual problems and womb infections, driven to eliminate these toxins either by masturbation or promiscuous sex acts. Parents today all too frequently do not realize how poor diet falsely stimulates the sex glands and sex drives of their children, or the harm that is done to the prostate in the male and the womb in the female, thus adversely affecting his or her future sex life.

Inability to maintain and sustain an erection in the male (impotence) as a result of prostate damage, lack of feeling in the vagina (frigidity) from acid sexual secretion in the female, or actual pain during the act of intercourse due to womb infection—almost all such physical problems can be eliminated by the use of a cleansing diet. Having the courage to be an individual, whether teenager or adult, and learning to maintain simple, lifelong, temperate habits of eating is not only good common sense, it's the way to good health. While most teenagers look for a leader to follow, the boy or girl who has the courage *to lead* can start a trend that will help the health of his or her friends.

It has been my experience that, once the teenage boy or girl is in an optimum state of health, his or her thinking clears up. The need for unnatural stimulation from dead food, drugs, cigarettes, or alcohol can then be confidently offset, and ultimately the need disappears.

To the growing boy, the adolescent years are equivalent to a passage through treacherous storms on the high seas. He has new pressures brought to bear from within and without. Adolescents are curious, stimulated from within by a growing sex urge and by the process of maturing. If the parents have fed their sons foodless food, high in salt content or white sugar, and fried starches, an inner pollution may result, and the toxins are thus forced to be eliminated vicariously through the male sex organs.

The problem of homosexuality can be acute in adolescence. For the teenage boy to know and understand how to handle any situation he may encounter it is advisable for him to understand that all human beings go through four stages of sexual development:

(1)   The earliest is the autoerotic, the self-pleasure stage, in which the infant is aware only of itself and its own sensations.

(2)   The first love awakening, or love for family, comes when the child recognizes his parents.

(3)   The homosexual stage, during which young people prefer the company of their own sex.

(4)   The heterosexual stage, the final stage, of love for the opposite sex usually culminates in marriage, home, and children.

Throughout all four stages it is necessary for the parents to remain alert to the importance of proper nutritional habits for their children. Parents can perform this valuable service by always recognizing the co-relationships of pure food and health and dead food and disease. During the child's teenage years, when a boy or girl has all he or she can do to handle growing sex urges in a body growing faster than can seemingly be kept up with, such recognition is especially important.

Teenage Toxemia

When a teenager is suffering from toxemia, so often derived from the unnatural stimulation of poor food, he may have trouble thinking straight, making clear-cut decisions. His system polluted, he's apt to be loggy, indifferent—perhaps rebellious because he's not feeling right—and is thus more easily drawn to the drug scene.

This is exactly what happened to a 16-year-old boy who became a patient of mine. His mother was divorced; he was an only child who had no father or father-figure in his life.

He started taking drugs in the seventh grade: marijuana, the amphetamines (such as Benzedrine and Dexamyl), and the barbiturates (sold as sleeping pills). By the time he was in the tenth grade, he had gone on at least two LSD trips.

This youth lived on hot dogs, cola drinks, tacos, white bread, and bologna. Most of the time he was so toxic he had no appetite at all. To compound his problems, during this period he met a 25-year-old dancer, also on drugs, who depleted him sexually.

When his mother finally discovered the truth, she decided to put him in a private boys' school. He promised her that he would stop taking all drugs. This declaration on his part, together with the belief that drugs would certainly not be permitted in a private boys' school, further assured the mother that he was cured of the habit and would keep his promise.

Then she discovered from another woman, whose boy was

also attending the same school, that most of the students smoked marijuana and that the den father was the pusher. She took her son out of that school. Back in public school, he became more of a problem. Most of his friends were older, and he identified with them. They were drop-outs, so he began to cut school; twice he was picked up by the police and brought to Juvenile Hall. The second time this happened, one of his companions had marijuana in his possession.

The boy's mother quit her job and moved him to another city, away from the influence of his friends. In his new environment, the same drug problem existed in school, but for a period of six months he was able to resist drugs. Finally, he smoked some marijuana, which resulted in a "bad trip." Suffering horribly, he went through all the symptoms of a bad LSD trip. His mother could scarcely keep from panicking. She told me later that he was delirious, that his heart was beating so loudly it seemed she could hear it from across the room.

There was a wall of anguish between mother and son when I met them. She wanted very much to trust him again but didn't know if she could. He was nervous, depleted, anxiety-ridden, and very disoriented. He was thin and gaunt. His urinalysis showed heavy uric acid and some kidney damage, apparently from drugs and toxic foods. His liver was swollen and his urine burned whenever he urinated.

I prescribed bed rest, as his adrenal glands were exhausted and he had very little energy. I put him on a clean diet—alkaline vegetables, potatoes, fruits (especially bananas and papayas), raw egg yolks, raw milk, small amounts of fish, lamb, and rare beef, cereal, honey and wheat-berry bread.

Six months later he had gained fifteen pounds and his urine indicated that his kidneys and liver were being rejuvenated. He had returned to school where, in a year's time, he became an honor-roll student. He graduated with honors from high school and is now in college. No longer craving unnatural stimulation from toxic drugs, his body is clean and he has acquired a new respect for himself.

Drugs and the Personality

The daily papers are filled with stories of murder and suicides that occur under the influence of drugs of one kind or another. Many times the personality of the teenager undergoes several changes due to the use of drugs. In a recent seminar, reported by the Los Angeles *Times,* Dr. Constandinos J. Miras, a pharmacologist from the University of Athens, recounted personality changes that chronic users of marijuana undergo. He defined a chronic user as one who smoked at least two marijuana cigarettes a day for two years or longer. "Then you begin to see the changes that typify the long-time user—the slowed speed, the lethargy, the lowered inhibitions and the loss of morality," Dr. Miras told the seminar.

One of the most striking characteristics is the loss of inhibition. "Marijuana users will accept a perfectly plausible thing which five years ago they did not even like to hear discussed. They will become suddenly violent without any apparent provocation. They will even kill," the pharmacologist said.

Dr. Miras' conclusions are based on twenty years of observation of chronic marijuana smokers in Greece. His most recent studies, which include the use of radioactive marijuana in tracking the course followed by the active ingredient THC (tetrahydrocannabinol) as it passes through the body, have been supported by the U.S. National Institute of Health. (Contrary to popular belief, THC is present in all parts of the marijuana plant: the stem, leaves, seeds, and flowering tops of both male and female plants.)

In a few long-time users who subsequently stopped using marijuana, Dr. Miras said that he had been able to detect the lethargy and loss of inhibition as long as two years after they had ceased—evidence indicating that marijuana may have a permanent organic effect on the brain.

Many of the human subjects Dr. Miras studied in Athens

were teachers and members of the arts. Gradually, as the years passed, a good number of them left their professions and slipped into other jobs, but they preferred most of all to "sleep and talk philosophy." "This is where the main danger is to our young people—the tendency to lose interest in ambition and drive: what will be the future of a nation whose young people have no interest in success?" he asked.

The studies, he said, have firmly established that marijuana does not promote sexuality. This theory is but a subjective impression based on the fact that the plant's ingredients lower inhibitions. Performance, however, is actually impaired.

Dr. David Smith, the Haight-Ashbury clinic's noted director, reported an interesting case illustrating the effects of long-term marijuana use on the sex life of a young man. He had been smoking "grass" intermittently for four years, then decided to turn on daily and drop out. He moved to Haight-Ashbury, where he cohabited with a girl, and lived what he described as a "very happy and anxiety-free" existence. Then came the bomb.

After a six-month period he noted he could not enjoy sex as before. At the time he first consulted the clinic, he had failed in having sexual relations with his girl for a period of three weeks. "He was persuaded to stop smoking marijuana on a trial basis," Smith reported. After he did so, his sex drive gradually returned and he could function normally once again.

Studies with radioactive THC have shown that the substance passes through the brain very quickly—in about twenty minutes. It concentrates in the liver and is passed into the intestines by way of the bile. Excretion takes at least five days.

Chronic users are prone to anemia, eye inflammation, and respiratory infections. There is also good evidence of abnormal brain-wave readings persisting for a year after the subject has given up the habit. THC appears to be both a stimulant and a depressant, and is difficult to test because of its uniqueness as a chemical compound. THC in the body of an experimentally pregnant animal appears to cross the placenta and enter the fetus.

To state categorically that pot has no detrimental physical or mental effects is to ignore some sixty papers appearing in current medical journals about this drug. These papers report liver damage in chronic users, acute delusional psychotic reactions in both casual and chronic users, deformed offspring occurring in cannabis-injected laboratory animals, disruption of educational programs, and social dropping-out.

The Harris-Isbell work done at the University of Kentucky showed that a "good reefer," containing from 3 to 6 milligrams of active ingredient (THC), could produce widespread autonomic and emotional reactions (as occurred in forty human volunteers), such as hallucination, depersonalization, and distortion of sight and hearing of so profound a nature as to be classified as a psychotic reaction.

A San Francisco Veterans Administration psychiatrist has blamed the heavy use of extra-strong Vietnamese marijuana by soldiers in southeast Asia for an excess of killings in the war and a high rate of mental illness among veterans. He based his report on studies of 2,041 Vietnam veterans in the course of two and a half years. He said that the heavy use of drugs by soldiers—LSD and amphetamines, as well as marijuana—is responsible for having caused a high rate of mental breakdown among Vietnam returnees.

The prolonged use of marijuana in teenagers sometimes leads to the use of LSD, lysergic acid derivatives. Lysergic acid diethylamide is one of the strongest drugs known to man. Lysergic acid is a natural product of an ergot fungus (Claviceps purpurea) which grows on rye and other grain. The action of this drug (and for that matter all psychotomimetics) is to cause alterations in mood, perception, and behavior. Death can result from LSD use, since the drug may induce respiratory failure. In addition, LSD can produce severe reactions in borderline psychotic and depressed patients.

Dr. Cecil B. Jacobson of George Washington University Medical School in Washington, D.C., told Congress recently that LSD can cause deformed babies, mutations of future generations, and premature aging of cells. Emphasizing that his findings were preliminary, Jacobson said, nonetheless, "the evidence is now rather substantial that chromosomal breakage occurs" in women who took LSD as well as in their offspring.

Dr. Jacobson said evidence was building that LSD or any other agent that causes chromosomes to break will shorten cell life. Jacobson said there was also evidence that LSD taken during pregnancy may result in abnormal babies. In addition, he stated, the drug could cause genetic changes that may not appear for several years or even generations.

Mescaline is another popular drug causing toxic reactions. It comes from mescal, a Mexican cactus (*Lophophora williamsii*), which contains the active hallucinogenic drug. The user experiences visual illusions and hallucinations closely resembling those of LSD, including acute anxiety and panic.

STP is a synthetic chemical related to the amphetamine family (Methedrine, Dexadrine) that produces psychic effects similar to mescaline but is some forty to fifty times more powerful than mescaline.

Heroin, an opiate, is generally in the form of a white powder and is a depressant. It can be sniffed or, more usually, taken by injection. When heroin is sniffed ("snorted," as the drug jargon goes), it has a bitter taste; therefore, heroin is usually injected in a vein. Most drug victims lose the ability, once the drug has taken hold, to tell how much they have absorbed, and they are therefore prone to overdose. Liver destruction in varying degrees is common among heroin addicts. The drug impairs or actually destroys the addict's chance for a sexually healthy life, if indeed he lives through the experience.

A Close Look at Tobacco

One of the greatest problems of all with the use of mind-altering drugs is that they can change a person without his actually being aware of it. Cigarettes, too, can have that effect.

Teenagers who smoke sometimes don't realize that they are forming a destructive habit pattern, one which is opposed to their physical well-being and emotional stability. And without physical well-being and emotional stability it is impossible to reap the benefits of sexual health.

The beginning teenage smoker often has symptoms of mild nicotine poisoning, dizziness, faintness, rapid pulse, and the cold clammy skin that is a symptom of liver malfunction. Sometimes nausea, vomiting, and diarrhea occur.

The major toxin in cigarettes is nicotine, a colorless, oily compound which, in concentrated form, is one of the most powerful poisons known. It is marketed as an insecticide under the trade name of Black Leaf 40. The injection of one drop, 70 milligrams, of Black Leaf 40 can cause the death of a man of average weight within a few minutes. The same amount placed on the gum of a dog will kill the dog. The nicotine content of cigarettes sold in this country ranges from about 0.5 milligrams per cigarette in some brands to 2 milligrams in others.

Some chemicals in tobacco tar—one of which is called phenol—first stop and then destroy the protective action of the cilia, the small hair-like projections that line the respiratory tract. Still others are irritants that cause the so-called cigarette cough and probably are responsible to a great extent for the gradual deterioration of lung tissue that results in emphysema. And every smoker absorbs some of the nicotine tar in cigarette smoke. Several studies have shown that ulcers of the stomach are five times as frequent, and ulcers of the duodenum twice as frequent, in cigarette smokers as in nonsmokers.

The most notable effect of nicotine is a transient stimulation followed by depression of both the sympathetic and the central nervous system. Nicotine causes a discharge of epinephrine from the adrenal glands, which in turn stimulates the nervous system and endocrine glands and causes the release of glycogen (sugar) from the liver. This results in a feeling of unnatural stimulation and relief from fatigue that, however, is transient and is followed by depression and further fatigue.

The bronchial tubes of the lungs have a remarkable protective mechanism. The cells lining these tubes and tubules secrete mucus, a sticky fluid that collects particles of soot, dust, and other substances in inhaled air. This mucus is carried up through the bronchial tubes and the trachea by the action of the cilia and is either swallowed or expectorated. The cilia maintain a continuous whiplike motion of about 900 beats a minute. Their movement causes mucus to flow up and out of the lungs. Particles of inhaled dust and other substances trapped in the mucus are thus removed, keeping the lungs clean and protecting the bronchial tubes from damage. If the cilia are destroyed or fail to work this protection is lost.

An analysis of respiratory diseases among 179 boys, 14 to 19 years of age, in a New Jersey preparatory school showed that severe respiratory illnesses were 9 times as frequent among regular smokers as among nonsmokers. In the case of occasional smokers, these illnesses were 2.6 times as common as with nonsmokers.

The heart rate increased after smoking. In one group of young people studied, the average increase after a single cigarette was twenty-one beats per minute. Occasionally, the heartbeat becomes irregular and there is pain in the chest. Blood pressure usually rises and may remain elevated for several hours.

Smoking brings epinephrine into the bloodstream, and this causes the small arteries to contract or become smaller. The flow of blood through these small vessels is cut down and the result is a lowering of the temperature of the skin. This occurs in habitual smokers as well as in teenagers who are just beginning to smoke. In a study of one hundred persons, the smoking of a single cigarette caused an average drop of 5.3° F. in the temperature of the fingers and toes. Smoking may sometimes impair liver function and circulation, causing cold extremities.

Some teenagers and adults think smoking tobacco or marijuana relieves fatigue. This may be because, as we have seen, nicotine causes a temporary increase of sugar in the blood, and more sugar means more fuel for the muscles. But after a brief time the fuel is used up, and the feeling of fatigue is greater than before.

Until thirty or forty years ago, smoking was limited almost exclusively to men. Teenage boys and occasionally girls experimented with cigarettes, but few smoked regularly. The few women who smoked did so in the privacy of their homes.

Today the situation is vastly different. According to the latest National Health Survey, 51 percent of the men and 33 percent of the women over 17 years of age are cigarette smokers. Breaking these statistics down further, it was determined that 48.6 percent of the males and 33.9 percent of the females in the 17-20-year-old group smoked regularly. In the 20-34-year-old group, the figure for males jumped to 60.7 percent and for the females to 43.5 percent.

In a large study, thousands of sections of lungs of smokers and nonsmokers who died from diseases not associated with smoking were examined microscopically. In these sections abnormal changes and thickening of the walls of the small branches of the bronchi and the alveoli were found regularly in smokers and very rarely in nonsmokers. According to another study, 93 percent of smokers had abnormal cells in their lungs but only 1.2 percent of nonsmokers did.

Another disease associated with cigarette smoking is emphysema. Dr. Roger S. Mitchell, specialist in diseases of the chest at the Webb-Waring Institute for Medical Research of the University of Colorado, has reported that 95 percent of emphysema patients, with a loss of 50 percent or more of their lung function, are heavy cigarette smokers. Studies also show that the death rate for chronic bronchitis and emphysema increases with the number of cigarettes smoked; for those smoking less than a pack a day, the death rate is five times as high as in nonsmokers, and for those smoking more than a pack a day the death rate is eight times as high.

Cirrhosis of the liver is shown by several studies to be about twice as frequent a cause of death in cigarette smokers as in nonsmokers.

Why do teenagers start to smoke? The answer is simple: the teenage boy and girl are susceptible to their peers; they want to be accepted.

As William Osler, M.D., stated in his essay on *Harvey and His Discovery:* "Sooner or later—insensibly, unconsciously—the iron yoke of conformity is upon our necks; and in our minds, as in our bodies, the force of habit becomes irresistible. From our teachers and associates [friends], from our reading, from the social atmosphere about us, we catch the beliefs of the day, and they become ingrained—part of our nature."

The matter of conformity perhaps has never been better expressed than in the famous lines that occurred to Henry Sidgwick in his sleep:

> We think so because all other people think so;
> Or because—or because—after all, we do think so;
> Or because we were told so, and think we must think so;
> Or because we once thought so, and think we still think so;
> Or because, having thought so, we think we still think so.

In departing from settled opinion or belief, the variation, the change, the break with custom may come gradually. The way is usually prepared, but the final break is made, as a rule, by some one individual who, to paraphrase Rudyard Kipling, sees with his own eyes and, with an instinct or genius for truth, escapes from the routine in which his fellows live.

It has been my experience with children who are brought up on a clean diet that they are usually not attracted to such toxic substances as cigarettes. Many of my teenage patients have told me that they have tried a cigarette and found the taste repulsive.

The best way to break the habit of cigarette smoking is to remain an individual and never start.

The Effects of Alcohol

Insofar as health is concerned, while the drinking of alcoholic beverages invariably is deleterious to both adult and teenager, more serious damages to youth may occur than to grownups. Ethyl alcohol can kill new, tender cells or maturing cells.

The drinking habit pattern generally starts in the teen years. Either friends give parties at which drinking occurs, or the teenager's family indulges in wine or cocktails at night. If one or both parents should have a chronic drinking pattern then there can be a real problem for the son or daughter, in the home and outside of it.

I was called in on the case of a teenage boy who first tried drinking when he was age 12. An older schoolmate gave him a Coke bottle half-filled with whiskey. He drank it on the school playground and promptly passed out. An ambulance was called and the boy's stomach was pumped at a nearby emergency hospital.

His father, a heavy social drinker, thought it was amusing. The boy's mother, a patient of mine, was horrified. A short time later the boy drank a large quantity of whiskey, straight, on a school athletic night, and again passed out. The boy's mother, by then separated from his father, was notified by the police to pick up her son at Juvenile Hall. Since he was under 18, he wasn't booked but released with a warning and left in the mother's custody.

When he was 16, he was involved in an automobile accident while under the influence of alcohol. Again he escaped confinement, because he was in the passenger's seat and not driving. The driver was killed, as were two other people, one a child in the second car involved in the accident.

The shock of the accident brought this youngster sufficiently to his senses so that he agreed to follow a cleansing regime I suggested. His mother followed the program with him; he became interested in sports and acquired a new set of friends. It took almost a year of rigid discipline on his part to rid himself of what appeared to be alcohol addiction and signs of liver damage.

The great majority of recovered alcoholics state that their preoccupation with drinking began early in their teenage careers. No party, football game, or social event was complete without drinking. Teenagers drink alcohol beverages chiefly to become stimulated. Actually, however, ethyl alcohol is a sedative. Teenagers driving under the influence of alcohol often find their space perception not functioning. As a result, according to a report, *You and Traffic Safety Education*, highway accidents cause approximately one-half of the deaths among youths from 15 to 21 years of age.

Dr. George Maddox, Chief of Medical Sociology at Duke University, recently made a survey of 2,000 students in three high schools. His findings were that at least 92 percent of high school students have sampled alcohol, 23 percent use it occasionally, and 6 percent, by their own classification, are frequent users.

Most teenage alcoholics, while drinking, suffer from malnutrition. Alcohol is a unique substance in that, unlike most drugs, it can serve as a fuel (but *not* a food) for the body. It is double-barreled in its activity, serving as a source of energy, like sugar, but at the same time acting as a poison to derange the appetite mechanisms, thereby offsetting the wish for food.

When treating a teenager with a drinking problem, I usually do a urinalysis to determine what harm may have been done to the vital organs. I interview the patient to determine if there are any emotional difficulties connected with his drinking. I try to get back to the cause and help with education, if I can. I prescribe an individual diet to cleanse the existing toxemia, and follow this with a new diet to rebuild the body.

It has been my experience that once the teenage boy or girl is in an optimum state of health, his or her thinking clears up. After that, the need for unnatural stimulation from dead food, drugs, cigarettes, or alcohol can be confidently offset, and ultimately the need disappears.

YOUR DIGESTION
AND YOUR SEX LIFE

Patients suffering from any one of a variety of diseases, such as diabetes or heart disease, or any of the other diseases that fill the pages of so many medical textbooks including impotence and frigidity, seem to share one common thought. What they have in common, in addition to a desire to get well and stay well, is the question: Why did this have to happen to me?

We live in such a complex civilization that few are ready to accept a simple answer. I believe and have proved, through my research in the study of colloid and endocrine chemistry and through countless experiences in the healing of many cases, that the primary cause of most disease is not germs. Disease is caused by toxemia, the presence of body poisons, which results in cellular impairment and breakdown in the body, thus paving the way for the onslaught and multiplication of germs. In my estimation, virtually every disease known to man can be cured through the proper use of correct food, neutralizing and eliminating the toxins from the system. Nature heals, if only we will have patience and cooperate with her. Most diseases are the result of years of toxic accumulation before they manifest as disease.

Inner pollution commences in a very devious way. It begins because of conditioned habit patterns in eating and drinking. Eating is, in itself, a social way of life. Eating has great significance in society; it is involved with religion, culture, belonging to a group. Eating habit patterns are established in childhood. Far too many children are allowed—in fact sometimes they're even taught—to eat such dead foods as ice cream, candy, cookies, and soda pop. Ironically, they are actually brain-washed into valuing these foods which produce the toxins that pollute their bodies and cause childhood diseases.

When the vicious circle of eating dead, toxin-producing foods continues, then disease of one kind or another tends to follow. During childhood, some—but only some—toxins are eliminated via various childhood diseases, such as measles, chickenpox, flu, colds, etc. By the time the child has grown into adulthood, therefore, his body cells may be saturated with toxic material.

The magnificent human body, sometimes described as a chemical engine that selects its own fuel, also builds and repairs itself and maintains quite a number of automatic chemical and electric control systems. We are able to walk, talk, make love, and perform work because of the energy we get from food. Within the limits of the menu at home, or in restaurants or the supermarkets, we usually can choose from a wide variety of fuels for our bodies. We have the responsibility of choice.

One time we may select something toxin-producing, like french fried potatoes and a chocolate soda, and the next time ham and eggs. Each food seems to go into the chemical engine with equal ease. If the energy output from one type of food is not as good as from another, we can raid the refrigerator and stoke a little more fuel into the engine. Eventually, of course, if we use the wrong fuel too many times, the engine will cease functioning properly . . . and disease is frequently the result.

What kinds of fuel should be chosen for this chemical engine?

Actually the human body can manufacture its own fuels if we provide the raw materials: carbohydrates, fats, proteins, minerals, vitamins, water, and roughage—every one of which is necessary.

These necessities can be obtained from the four basic food groups. Here are the four groups and some of the best fuels to be had within each group: the meat group, including rare beef, rare lamb, fish, eggs and poultry; the milk group, raw cow's or goat's milk; the vegetable/fruit group including leafy green vegetables, potatoes, zucchini, etc.; and the bread/ cereals group.

If we are to understand how the body is given energy then we must understand how the digestive system works.

The Digestive Process

The first section of the digestive canal is in the mouth. Here the food is subjected to five procedures. It is tested by the sense organs, cut up into smaller pieces by the teeth, treated chemically by the saliva, formed into a bolus by the tongue, and swallowed by means of the muscles of the esophagus.

Three sense organs—eye, nose, and tongue—participate in testing the food. The eye is a long-distance apparatus. It examines an object at a distance and determines whether or not it belongs to the category of food. After the eye has recognized the substance as food, the nose tests it for edibility. It determines whether meat is fresh or spoiled— unless the person is so toxic that his sense of smell is off and he finds it difficult to distinguish spoiled from fresh meat.

After this second examination, the food is placed in the mouth where the tongue determines its taste. Not only are the impressions received by the sense organs decisive for the acceptance or rejection of food; they also act internally as "starters", cranking up the digestive organs by way of the nervous system.

In the mouth, the food is crushed and chopped by the

teeth, which are brought together by the powerful forces of the jaw muscles.

The tongue itself is comprised of muscles. The tongue muscles can change the shape of that organ, making its surface convex or concave. They also raise or lower the tongue and move it from side to side to assist in chewing food. On the surface of the tongue are sense organs called taste buds, which detect four taste sensations: sweet, sour, salty, and bitter.

Even the teeth have specialized jobs in preparing food for digestion. The incisors and canine teeth, at the front of the jaws, cut and tear food into smaller pieces. The molars, at the rear, grind the food.

While food is being pulverized into the pulpy mass called a bolus, the digestive juice of the salivary glands begins a breakdown of the carbohydrates. An enzyme in the saliva, ptyalin, splits the molecules of starch into smaller molecules of sugar. In addition to the digestive action of the ptyalin, the fluid of the salivary glands serves several other purposes. Saliva provides moisture needed by the taste buds. It also has a cleansing action on the teeth, and it washes away food particles that otherwise might provide a home for bacteria.

The salivary glands look like bunches of tiny grapes. The largest, the parotid, is located in front of the ear. Two salivary glands in the lower jaw are the sublingual, under the tip of the tongue, and the submandibular, under the edge of the lower jaw.

Now the bolus of food, thoroughly chewed, is ready to be passed into the stomach by swallowing. The muscles of the cheeks, the tongue, and the roof of the mouth form a chute. The tongue presses upward and backward against the hard palate. This moves the bolus of food toward the back of the mouth and into the pharynx, the common passageway for both food going to the stomach and air going to the lungs. The soft palate is raised as the food passes toward the back of the mouth; this closes the opening to the nasal cavities. At the same time, the epiglottis—a lid made of cartilage enclosed in mucous membranes and located at the base of the tongue over the larynx at the top of the wind-pipe—closes. Also simultaneously, the larynx moves upward against the lower surface of the epiglottis. This seals off the windpipe at the instant of swallowing. But, as we all know, if our timing is off, some food or water may get into the larynx. When this happens, a coughing reflex is triggered.

Part of the cause of inner pollution can be attributed to carbohydrates that were not properly masticated in the mouth. It is therefore very important that we chew our food thoroughly, since carbohydrate digestion chiefly takes place in the mouth. Carbohydrates swallowed without proper mastication ferment in the stomach and intestines, causing gas and certain toxemias.

After the food enters the esophagus, it passes into the portion of the digestive system that is controlled by the smooth, or involuntary, muscles. The previous actions—chewing and swallowing—were performed by striated, or voluntary, muscles. When food reaches the esophagus, it is moved along by muscle action, called peristalsis, which is carried out by involuntary muscles. The digestive tube has two layers of involuntary muscles, the inner layer forming a series of circles about the tube. When any of these muscle fibers contract, the tube becomes smaller at that point. The outer muscle layer is longitudinal, its fibers running the length of the tube, and contracting as the circular muscles relax. The alternate contraction and relaxation of the two sets of muscles push food along the digestive tube in peristaltic waves. (Because of the peristaltic action of the muscles in the esophagus, it is possible to drink a glass of water while standing on your head.) Then, at the end of the esophagus, the food reaches the cardiac sphincter, at the entrance to the stomach.

The stomach is a J-shaped organ about ten inches long, lying below a sheet of muscle fibers and fibrous tissue called the diaphragm. The diaphragm stretches across the body cavity at the level of the bottom of the rib cage. When a person vomits, the diaphragm pushes down against the stomach as the abdominal muscles contract. This overall squeezing of the stomach forces out its contents, with the help of reverse waves of peristalsis. The walls of the stomach are very muscular. They contain not only layers of circular and longitudinal muscle fibers, but a third layer of oblique muscle fibers. The muscles are particularly important for the stomach because it is the job of this organ to break up the food into tiny particles. It must be remembered that if the food is not chewed properly, the stomach is overworked, which upsets the digestive system.

The mucous membrane that lines the entire digestive system is thick and velvety and has many folds. Like other mucous membranes, the lining contains mucous glands. But in the stomach, between the mucous glands, are tiny gastric glands which secrete digestive juices. The lining of the stomach contains about 35 million glands.

In aiding the digestive process the stomach's gastric glands secrete hydrochloric acid and several enzymes. One enzyme, *rennin*, helps to digest milk. Another enzyme, *lipase*, splits certain fats, including those in cream and egg yolk. The hydrochloric acid combines with proteins to form a new chemical. A third enzyme, *pepsin*, splits the chemical formed by the proteins and hydrochloric acid into smaller units. The pepsin also digests the milk curds formed by the rennin.

Since the acid and enzymes in the stomach can digest meat, why isn't the stomach itself digested? Small amounts of ammonia are secreted by cells in the lining of the stomach, this chemical counteracting the effects of normal amounts of hydrochloric acid. Excess acid from the stomach's gastric glands, however, can result in ulcers in certain areas of the stomach and the small intestine.

The time taken for a meal to be changed by the stomach into a semifluid called chyme varies from about three to five hours. Fluids, as might be expected, pass through the stomach within minutes. Carbohydrates, among the solid foods, are digested chiefly in the mouth and small intestines.

The process takes approximately one hour. Proteins take a longer time, meat sometimes twelve hours. Fats require the most time. Some fats, in fact, retard the digestive process for other foods by slowing down the secretion of the gastric juices.

The pyloric sphincter at the lower end of the stomach controls the emptying of chyme into the next section of the digestive route, the small intestine. Like the cardiac sphincter between the esophagus and the stomach, the pyloric sphincter is a thickened band of circular muscles. Waves of peristalsis push the chyme through the opening formed by the pyloric sphincter and into the small intestine.

The small intestine is so named because of the diameter of its tube, only one half inch. It is about twenty feet in length, about four times longer than the large intestine. The first portion of the small intestine is a short horseshoe-shaped section known as the duodenum, into which enter digestive juices including chyme. Also added to the chyme are fluids from the pancreas and bile from the liver. The pancreatic fluid contains a number of enzymes that act upon all kinds of foods: proteins are broken down into amino acids, large sugar molecules are changed to simple sugars, and fats are reduced to fatty acids in preparation for absorption into the blood or lymph vessels.

Insulin is secreted by the pancreas also, but it is absorbed directly into the blood. There it is used by the digestive juices. When the pancreas is unable to supply insulin to the body, diabetes results.

Bile enters the duodenum through a duct either directly from the liver or from the gall bladder, and is stored in the latter. Though normal bile is composed mostly of water, it contains pigments from destroyed red blood cells. These pigments undergo chemical changes in the intestine and eventually are excreted, giving the yellow-brown color to feces. The iron from these cells is reabsorbed, however. Bile also contributes to digestion by emulsifying fatty foods and making them easier to absorb. Bile also reduces the acidity of the chyme. The bile is additionally an excretory product of the liver, and can be very toxic and acid at times, depending on the diet.

Beyond the duodenum there is about eight feet of small intestine called the jejunum, and beyond that is about twelve feet of intestine known as the ileum. The diameter of the small intestine gradually decreases along its length. At the junction of the small and large intestine the bore is about an inch and a half, half the diameter of the duodenum; the cecum, where the two intestines meet, is about three inches broad.

The interior of the small intestine is carpeted with microscopic finger-like projections called villi. The cells which cover the villi permit the absorption of water and the final products of digestion into the vessels that carry away the blood and lymph. Small amounts of digestion products are absorbed through the walls of the stomach but most of the molecules of sugars, amino acids, and fat products are absorbed through the millions of villi in the small intestine. The villi are in constant motion, swinging back and forth and changing in length. This motion keeps the chyme thoroughly mixed with the digestive juices while molecules of food pass through the cells on the surface of the villi. Fat products generally enter lymph vessels in the villi, while sugars and amino acids enter blood capillaries.

The blood vessels carry the food products to the liver while the lymph vessels move their food units into a duct emptying into the subclavian vein, near the top of the rib cage.

After traveling along this chemical refinery's conveyor belt to the end of the small intestine, about all that remains of a meal is water and waste products. The chyme passes into the large intestine through a valve that prevents a backflow into the small intestine. The large intestine, about five feet long, has the general shape of a picture frame as it runs upward, across, and down through the abdominal cavity. It has no villi and fewer folds than are observed in the small intestine.

Much of the water is absorbed through the walls of the

large intestine. The waste products form the semisolid feces that are excreted through the rectum. Some waste products, including salts and proteins, are filtered from the blood, along with excess water, by a series of tubules in the kidneys. This waste is excreted as urine.

ORGANS
OF ELIMINATION

7

In the normally functioning body, the wastes resulting from the digestive process are eliminated by organs specifically designed by Nature. These organs of elimination are the liver, the kidneys, and the skin.

The Liver

The most important organ of elimination is the liver. The reddish-brown liver manufactures proteins, processes carbohydrates, absorbs fat products and makes them available as fuel, serves as a storehouse for vitamins and minerals, treats iron for use in the blood system, and renders harmless some of the poisons that enter the bloodstream. It also dispatches sugars to the tissues to be utilized as body fuel.

The liver is the largest gland of the body. It weighs about three pounds on the average and fills the upper part of the abdomen under the right half of the diaphragm. Biochemists, perhaps the most prominent being Albert Szent-Györgyi, have recognized its great importance and have written abundantly about it.

This large organ has many functions. It is the manufacturing center of the enzymes and antigens and antitoxins of the body, as well as the site where most of the vitamins and organic salts and trace elements are prepared for use by the human system. Besides all this, it strains toxic and needless substances out of the venous blood as the blood returns from the digestive area of the bowel; it also seizes upon the beneficial products, from which it synthesizes the chemicals needed for general body metabolism. The elements it strains out are neutralized and converted into bile, which is the secretion carrying off the liver's excretory products.

In this chemical interaction, sodium, Nature's chief alkaline element, is extensively used. Nearly all of the neutralization products are sodium compounds. Many of the neutralized poisons from the body's digestion and metabolism come under the heading of sodium cholates, cholic acid being one of the bile's constituents. As long as the sodium reserves in the liver are available, the liver can perform its function as a blood-strainer. Completely strained blood resulting from a balanced clean food diet is nontoxic and normal. When the body circulates clean blood, it is impossible for disease, as we define it, to develop.

It has long been known that the liver creates heat. It remained for the great father of pediatrics, Abraham Jacobi, to recognize that during a fever in which the thermometer registered over 103°F. under the tongue, the temperature of the liver within the body was often 110°F. or more.

During normal, nondiseased states, the liver is the furnace that warms the blood. We might compare the liver to a hot-water furnace that circulates the hot water through the pipes and radiators in the various rooms of a house. As long as the furnace is adequate, all the rooms are comfortable. If there is insufficient fire in the furnace, it becomes necessary to close several rooms of the house. Similarly, when the liver becomes impaired as a furnace, parts of the body become cold, most often the hands and feet. Chilly extremities often indicate impaired liver function.

It must be noted that before oxidation of any kind is possible in the body, there must be adequate adrenal gland function. The thyroid is also of much importance. To follow the analogy, the carbohydrates are the fuel; the adrenals say whether the fire can burn or not; and the thyroid says how fast the fire burns. Adrenal secretion is so important in this burning process that the special organs of oxidation in the body—the liver and kidneys—histologically show small islands of extra adrenal tissue, called cell nests or cell rests, that help facilitate oxidation. In a normally functioning liver, both the adrenal glands and the adrenal cell rests supply enough of what De Sajous termed "adrenoxidase" to make complete oxidation of carbohydrates possible. Which means the gradual burning of a complex, large molecule carbohydrate to its end products: carbon dioxide (CO_2) and water (H_2O).

This oxidation of the liver can be visualized as follows: The fire does not produce flames but is a slow process, a few atoms being burned at a time. Some carbohydrates are very complex starches with a large number of carbon atoms to the molecule, but the proportion of hydrogen and oxygen (which burns the carbon, providing adrenoxidase is present) is generally two hydrogen atoms to one oxygen atom, as in the formula for water, H_2O. This proportion is generally maintained until the end products, CO_2 and H_2O, are reached. The CO_2, being a gas, is expelled through the lungs while the H_2O, called "metabolic" water, is eliminated through the kidneys.

Now the oxidation of carbohydrates that occurs in the liver, being a slow flameless fire, takes place in steps, a few carbon atoms being separated and burned at a time. For example, visualize a stairway, every step of which is the location of a new level of oxidation. As the complex starch in the carbohydrate is gradually oxidized ("burned"), new compounds result at each step of the oxidation process; such compounds run the gamut of organic mixtures, the most common being organic acids, ketones, aldehydes, and polyatomic alcohols, to name a few. The nomenclature is complex and belongs in the realm of organic chemistry—a field for the biochemists and scarcely the medical doctor. Yet it is overwhelmingly important that the practicing physician has a general idea of this complexity, for it is he who is called to help repair any disturbance of the complicated oxidation function.

As long as there is no break in the reaction chain, no broken or missing step, the oxidation process flows smoothly; most of the products arising from the slow burning of carbohydrates, exceedingly poisonous, are disposed of through the normal avenues of elimination.

When a break in the process does occur, it is usually the result of an impairment to the liver cells caused by heavy or prolonged use of refined sugar and starch. As a consequence of this break in the chain, the normal eliminative process is most likely to be side-stepped and the toxic compounds may then circulate directly into the general blood flow. This results in a pathological condition which could harm or destroy body tissues.

The avenues of vicarious elimination controlled by the endocrine glands, especially the thyroid gland (skin, mucous membranes, serous membranes) and the adrenal glands (bowels, kidneys, lungs, lymphatics), try to expel this toxic poison. In the attempt at vicarious elimination, considerable damage can be done to the tissues along the path taken by the poison.

For example, if the adrenals divert the vicarious elimination through the lungs, the result might be anything from mild bronchitis to lethal pneumonia. If the vicarious elimination takes place via the skin under control of the thyroid, a multitude of "skin diseases" could occur. Since there could be many lesions, depending on just where the break in the chain or steps occur, the nomenclature could fill a thick textbook in dermatology. I sincerely hope the time will come when the medical profession will realize the value of considering treatment of a so-called disease at its source and not concentrate on using the modern palliative treatment of either stimulating or depressing the endocrine glands, especially the adrenals and thyroid. Many toxic products have already been isolated and named, including pyruvic acid, acetic acid, aceto-acetic acid, diacetic acid, and sugar which gives rise to diabetes. These simpler products of toxemia occur near the end of the oxidation chain or steps.

Now, what causes the damage to the chain or its steps?

Our Caveman Liver

One very important fact to remember is that, although we still have the caveman's liver, we have strayed far from the caveman's diet. As food and *only* food builds the blood and the body, food certainly must be important in the maintenance of body health. During the past hundreds of years the innovations concocted by cooks, chefs and chemists have given us substances very irritating to our "caveman" liver. Starches, for example, have been synthesized, preserved, frozen, chemicalized, colored with aniline dyes, cooked, toasted, sweetened, and almost ruthlessly mixed up with acids, alkalies, and salts.

How can (refined white) sugar, which is a carbohydrate, be classified as a food when damage to the teeth, bones, lungs, liver, kidneys, joints, nerves, and brain (to mention only a few organs) may result from our ingesting it? Even honey is boiled, strained, refined, colored. Some claim *all* sugar is detrimental to the teeth, which is not so; the children of aboriginal tribes, who grow up gnawing sugar cane, have unusually healthy and beautiful teeth.

The liver has many other functions. Complex proteins are broken down and resynthesized in its nitrogenous metabolism similar to the carbohydrate chain oxidation process. Remembering that the caveman's liver was modeled to digest raw meat, we can easily understand what damage can be done by cooking, and especially *overcooking*, protein foods. In addition, much present-day meat is chemicalized, colored, preserved, embalmed, salted, frozen, sugar-cured, smoke-cured, greased, and canned. Little wonder, then, that liver damage causing neuritis, arthritis, tumors—to name but three possibilities—can occur.

Fat metabolism is another important liver function. Since fats are hydrocarbons they can either be changed to carbohydrates or burned directly as fats. Consider how many unnatural fats are ingested by modern man. The natural fats are limited to butterfat, some seed and nut oils, meat fats (excepting hog fat, which is unnatural because of the force-fed diet that results in fatty degeneration of the hog), and fruit fats (avocado, for example). A "fat injury" to the liver can cause acne, boils, pimples, carbuncles, fatty degeneration of various organs, pemphigus, and cancer.

The liver function also can be upset by many "foreign" foods and drinks, such as coffee, tea, chocolate, soft drinks, carbonated drinks, salt, condiments, spices, monosodium glutamate—to name a few.

In the liver food is reconstructed, foreign protein being converted into human protein. When in the intestinal canal, the protein of, for example, cow's milk is broken down, and rebuilt by the liver into human protein. If foreign proteins or protein derivatives are injected into the human body intravenously, there follows a reaction that varies from a mild rise in temperature to a state of extreme shock associated with collapse of the vasomotor regulation of the circulatory system. Even the products formed in the intestine during digestion—the peptones, for example—may have an action of this kind when injected into the blood. By remaking these proteins into usable form before permitting them to get into the bloodstream, the liver saves our lives daily.

Poisons such as nicotine, caffeine, morphine, and atropine are transformed into harmless compounds by the cellular protoplasm of the liver. Bacilli are caught and eaten by the liver cells. These achievements can be proved by numerous experiments. If a solution of soap is injected into an animal's blood system above the liver, the animal dies; if an equal quantity is injected into the portal vein so the soap solution must pass through the liver, nothing happens to the animal. The liver turns the soap into fat—fat usable by the animal. If a fatal dose of atropine is injected into the general circulation of an animal, it dies of atropine poisoning. Yet four times as much atropine can be injected into the portal vein of an animal and it will remain alive.

If a person drinks a large quantity of alcohol, the liver swells soon thereafter. Excessive imbibition of alcohol may, over a long period, produce a liver as hard as a board. Many habitual drinkers have sick livers because they partake of large amounts of alcoholic beverages, which are poisonous and damage the liver cells.

The liver cell is one of the most industrious and capable cells of the body. It is virtually incomprehensible how a microscopically small dot—100,000 cells could find room within a bread crumb—can carry on simultaneously so many and such diverse functions as the breakdown and reconstruction of carbohydrates, protein, and fats; chemical processes of the most complex kind such as the detoxification of poisons; the capture and digestion of bacilli and blood cells; and the production of highly active extracts and hormones.

From the substances it removes from the blood, the liver cell manufactures the digestive fluid, bile. Bile—or gall, as it is commonly known—is not a ferment. It is the only digestive juice that contains no enzyme. Fresh bile is a golden yellow fluid that rapidly loses its color when exposed to the air, turning dark green. Its bitter taste is responsible for the expression, "as bitter as gall." Bile contains two pigments, bilirubin (bile red) and biliverdin (bile green), which the liver prepares from the pigment of the blood, and also two bile acids which are actually the active components of the bile. These acids have three functions: (1) activating the enzyme of the pancreas, (2) emulsifying fat, and (3) making the fat droplets sticky.

The presence of bile in the intestine is necessary for the

normal absorption of fat. If the supply of bile is cut off by occlusion of the bile ducts, the utilization of fat drops from about 98 percent to 40 percent. After being emulsified, the fat is absorbed from the intestine and passes into the lymph vessels. A few hours after a meal rich in fats the intestinal lymphatics may be seen to be distended with the milky fluid, chyle. From the lymphatics the chyle passes into the thoracic duct, the main lymph trunk of the body, and from there into the bloodstream.

The bile does not flow directly from the liver into the intestine, but first into the gallbladder, a bag shaped like a tobacco pouch and attached to the lower surface of the liver. It holds approximately 30 to 35 cubic centimeters of fluid. The bile duct connects it with the intestine. This duct is usually closed, but when a small quantity of digested food passes the point where the duct opens into the intestine, it presses on a nerve switch. The gallbladder contracts, the bile duct opens, and a portion of bile flows over the food.

The gallbladder is a dispensable organ. (Many animals have no gallbladder—for instance, the horse, elephant, camel, deer.) As is well known, stones form quite easily in the human gallbladder. At the age of 30, one person in a hundred has gallstones, at 50 one in ten, and at 65 every fifth person—but not everyone with stones suffers because of them. Gallstones come to the attention of the individual only when they hinder the normal flow of bile and cause pain. If a stone becomes incarcerated in the narrow duct connecting the gallbladder with the intestine, a violent spasm or gallstone colic is produced. The bile collects in the liver and passes into the blood. As a result the affected person acquires a greenish-yellow color; he is jaundiced. Gallstones can become as large as a hen's egg, yet they are often so small the gallbladder may contain as many as two hundred.

The Kidneys

In the process of elimination, after the liver come the kidneys. The kidneys' function is to maintain in balance, in the blood, the water consumed by mouth and the metabolic water in the body.

The kidneys are two chocolate-colored, bean-shaped organs, each as large as a fist, suspended just under the diaphragm in the small of the back, technically in the lumbar region on the posterior wall of the abdomen. They are not enclosed in the abdomen's lining, the peritoneum, like the stomach, liver, or intestine, but hang with relative looseness near the spinal column; consequently they have a tendency "to sink down." If the ligaments that hold them in place become relaxed the kidneys tend to move around. Lying against the upper poles of the kidneys, perched on them like caps, are the adrenal glands.

The much-abused kidneys are among the most complex organs in the body. Even when literally over-burdened with toxemia they labor heroically until finally overwhelmed. When overwhelmed, uremic poisoning and congestive heart failure can result.

Physicians, engineers, and mechanics are best able to appreciate the kidneys as the marvelous filtering devices they are. Although small enough to fit in the palm of your hand, each kidney is equipped with a million individual chemical filter units. Each kidney, too, can filter seventeen hundred quarts of viscous fluid within twenty-four hours. The kidney, determining which chemicals are needed by the body, reabsorbs these and eliminates the unneeded ones.

Three divisions are seen in the cross-section of a kidney. The outer zone is a dark red color and is about one half to three quarters of an inch wide. This division contains tiny globes, each at the end of a small artery (arteriole), that filter the water from the blood. The middle division, lightest in color, consists of a meshwork of fine tubules, surrounded by minute veins (venules). These tubes carry the water, which has been filtered, to a central drainage area. The third or inner division, called the pelvis of the kidney, is a reservoir that drains through a long tube (ureter) into the bladder. The first two divisions contain no sensory nerves and thus cannot register pain when disordered. The third division, the kidney pelvis, is lined with cells that are richly supplied with sensory nerves and can register pain from kidney stones, or excessive acidity or alkalinity of the urine. Similarly equipped, and also sensitive, are the ureter and bladder.

The kidney receives its blood supply from arteries that branch from the abdominal aorta, the main artery that descends from the heart. The kidneys' main blood supply is thus arterial, the cleanest, reddest blood in the body. (It will be remembered that the blood supply of the liver is almost entirely venous, the most impure and bluest of blood.)

One of the chief functions of the kidney is to rid the blood of excessive water. Metabolic water is one of the two end products of carbohydrate metabolism; the other is carbon dioxide gas, which is eliminated through the lungs. Since the filtration of water through the tiny globes of the kidney is dependent upon blood with a high oxygen content, Nature has arranged for the supply of arterial blood—richest in oxygen.

A normal, healthy person has about a million globules in each kidney. Experiments on animals have shown that complete health can be maintained on one-fourth of the total kidney substance and that under such circumstances the animal's blood pressure remains normal. In the case of man the filtration is being done by roughly 250,000 globules. When a steady chemical destruction of globules occurs, blood pressure and heart problems can begin.

Although it has long been known that high blood pressure was in some way related to impaired kidney function, it was scientifically demonstrated by Dr. Harry Goldblatt of Cleveland. In his researches, Dr. Goldblatt proved three things: (1) that the blood pressure became elevated when there was an interference with the rate of blood flow through the kidneys; (2) that this elevation of pressure was possible only when the adrenal glands were not able to perform emergency duty, and (3) that once the state of high blood pressure was produced, none of the commonly used remedies for lowering it were efficacious.

Dr. Goldblatt's experiments proved that elevated blood pressure ensues when there is interference with blood circulation through the globules. Globules that have been destroyed by disease retard blood circulation. Nature elevates the pressure to ensure a sufficient blood supply through the remaining globules.

The most common irritants that cause degeneration of the globules are salt, toxic protein acids resulting from protein indigestion, metals like mercury, and drugs. When degeneration takes place the urine is composed mostly of pure water, since the weakened kidneys are unable to secrete the usual electrolytes (salts) and toxins.

The globules normally secrete only water and tubules conduct this water to the bladder for elimination. But, just as the globules can become diseased by improper chemistry, so also can the tubules be destroyed. However, before tubular pathology can be understood, we must briefly examine tubular physiology.

The function of the tubule, or nephron, is to conduct water from the globule toward the ureter which carries it to the bladder. These tubules are able to reabsorb water if it is needed to maintain a normal balance in the body cells. The tubules are long, to give plenty of surface for reabsorption; they are also surrounded by a minute network of veins.

When these veins contain diffusible acids, resulting from improper digestion of foods or poor oxidation of sugars and starches, the toxic elements can cause a serious condition. Either acute or chronic tubular disease may result. In acute form, tubular breakdown will cause blood and much albumen to be present in the urine. If the tubules should be completely destroyed, stoppage of urine results, followed rapidly by death.

In a number of chronic diseases, varying amounts of albumen, red cells, and casts are found in the tubules. The casts are composed of the lining cells of the tubules. They can be clear or hyaline (gelatin-like), fine or coarsely granular, waxy, or bloody. As the toxins trickle downward through the tubule, the concentration of toxic material increases.

At the tubule's end, or what is called the lower nephron, the toxins can become so concentrated that they may destroy the lower nephron and thus, in fact, even terminate life. This condition is diagnosed as a lower-nephron nephrosis, often seen in medical practice. When a patient becomes toxic, globules as well as tubules can be involved in a destructive process; therefore, it is unusual to see either a purely globular or purely tubular nephrosis.

Sometimes the toxic material in the vein, resulting from imperfect filtration of the venous blood by the liver (itself damaged by toxins), reaches a concentration high enough to cause severe inflammation of the vein. But when the arterial blood contains abnormal impurities, due very often to improper diet, to force elimination the kidneys need extra oxygen—this additional oxygen being supplied by the adrenal glands through an internal secretion (adrenoxidase).

When blood in the vein clots, the resultant catastrophe is known as phlebitis. The clot may break loose and float within the circulation, perhaps finally plugging the opening of a blood vessel. This results in what is called an infarct, destruction of the tissues normally fed by the blood vessel, now blocked. A continued plugging of the vessel causes an anemic area in the region supplied by the stopped-up vessel, and often a necrosis, or even death, can result.

Through a careful study of the urine, the character of the toxemia can be determined, often long before great destruction has been done. Then a curative diet, according to the individual's body type and the disease, can be prescribed. The diet gradually relieves the kidney of the burden that has forced the body to find avenues of vicarious elimination.

With the exceptions of sodium chloride (table salt) and certain poisonous drugs, the chief kidney irritants, according to my research, originate from improper digestion of proteins, carbohydrates, or hydrocarbons (fats).

I recently treated a case of hypertension (high blood

pressure). The man's pressure was up to 260/110. His urine was cloudy with sulfates and salt crystals. The history of the patient disclosed the fact that he had consumed far too much protein during most of his life.

I prescribed bed rest and a diet consisting mainly of dietetic antidotes. The following elements *in the form of vegetable broths* were then prescribed: sodium chloride, sodium carbonate, sodium phosphate, sodium iodide, sodium fluoride, sodium bromide, sodium silicate, and sodium borate. (In vegetables these minerals are all found in organic form.) Potassium was given in similar combinations; calcium as calcium carbonate, chloride, and phosphate; iron as chlorophyll compounds. Many trace elements and vitamins are always present in the above.

In a period of six months this therapy, consisting of useful nonirritating and antidotal elements, all organic in nature, had reduced the patient's blood pressure to normal; his urine was clear, indicating the kidneys had repaired themselves.

For patients with hypertension and liver or kidney damage, or both, I suggest rest in bed from five to seven days. If the blood pressure drops to 120/80, it means that the inflammatory state of the globules has been reduced and that the globules have returned to normal function as a result of the antidote food therapy. But suppose that, after from five to seven days, there is a drop only to 210/110. That means there has been a great deal of irreversible globular damage.

As we have seen, the liver and the kidneys are important natural eliminative organs. For the liver, the natural avenue of elimination is through the bowel; for the kidneys, through the bladder and urethra. However, when the liver is congested and cannot perform its eliminative function, waste matter (toxins) is thrown into the bloodstream. Similarly, when the kidneys are inflamed, toxins are dammed up in the blood.

Toxic blood must discharge its toxins or the person dies. Nature therefore uses vicarious or substitute avenues of elimination. The lungs will take over the task of eliminating some of the wastes that should have gone through the kidneys, or the skin will take over for the liver. The lungs obviously do not make good kidneys. From the irritation caused by elimination of poisons through this vicarious channel, bronchitis, pneumonia, or asthma may be caused, as determined by the particular chemistry of the poison being eliminated.

Skin

The skin receives one third of all the blood circulating throughout the body. In addition to elimination, this organ performs a number of important functions. Among these are the protection of the body against invasion of bacteria, against injury to the more sensitive tissues within the body, against the rays of the sun, and against the loss of body moisture.

The skin also serves as an organ of perception for the nervous system, and as a temperature regulator. For instance, when the surrounding air is considerably warm the skin is cooled by a compensating moisture secreted by its sweat glands.

The sebaceous (oil producing) glands and sweat glands are located deep in the skin's inner layers, and many, though not all, are connected to hair follicles. In each sebaceous gland are found from two to six lubules which each day produce a tiny amount of the oily substance sebum. Sebum, which is normally excreted at a steady rate regardless of weather conditions and other factors, acts as a means of eliminating dead skin cells being cast off by the system. Carrying the worn-out cells to the surface of the skin for disposal, sebum emerges virtually invisible from the ducts as a semi-liquid mixture of oil, toxic water and dead skin cells.

Perspiration, the skin's chief product of elimination, is mostly water (between 98 and 99 percent). Perspiration eliminates (in addition to water) toxic salts, organic acids, and small amounts of minerals the body no longer requires and which the body finds difficult to excrete through the urine. If these toxins and chemicals were not carried away naturally, a serious imbalance would be caused in the body's fluid composition and we could become ill.

The sweating function, a complex process, gives off a daily volume of perspiration of about one quart per day for the average adult in very cold weather, possibly two quarts on warm days. Output increases greatly under heavy exertion or mental stress.

Thus our skin is not only a protector against exterior materials and forces; it also plays a very important role in ridding the human system of inner deleterious chemicals and substances.

BODY TYPES AND ORGANS OF VICARIOUS ELIMINATION

The word *vicarious,* from the Latin word *vicarius,* means "substituted." The physiological definition reads: "denoting or pertaining to the performance of one organ or part of the functions normally belonging to another." In other words, other avenues of elimination are brought into play in support of lagging liver and kidney functions.

When the digestive system has been disturbed and the function of the natural eliminative organs (the liver and kidney) is impaired, other vital organs such as the pituitary gland, thyroid gland, adrenal glands, the inner or outer skin, and the heart take over and pinch-hit for the natural eliminative organs. The prostate in the male and the womb in the female also are avenues of vicarious elimination that might be forced to pinch-hit to help rid the body of toxins. Thus are avenues of vicarious elimination opened.

Doctors in ancient times used a system of body classification based on a person's form (thin or fat) or according to his temperament (choleric, phlegmatic, sanguineous, melancholic—terms we still use today). Hippocrates classified man according to blood, phlegm, and color of the bile; he instructed his students to observe body structure to make accurate diagnoses.

There are those observers who have devised various systems of using body build—"somatyping"—in a hopeful attempt to fit all men into tight little categories. Dr. William H. Sheldon, in his exhaustive *Atlas of Men*, correlated body types into three overall classes: the fleshy endomorphs, the muscular mesomorphs, and the thin ectomorphs. But such classifications do not tell us much about individual differences, differences each of us obtains from the huge and unique assortment of genes.

It remained for a rather new science, endocrinology (from two Greek words meaning "within" and "separate"), to give us a new method of classifying human beings. The ancients made groping attempts to understand the functions of the important endocrine glands, but only after painstaking work during the past fifty years has endocrinology begun to unlock the mysteries of these glands. And since, virtually from birth, the endocrine secretions (called hormones, from the Greek "to arouse") play a most important role in determining the physical and neurological types of individuals we will become, it follows that endocrinology offers the best approach to typing us physiologically as well.

Though a complete understanding of endocrinology remains somewhere in the future, individuals and families, even races and nations, show definite internal-secretion traits that stamp them with particular racial, national, family, and physical characteristics, as well as individual qualities that differentiate them from others.

Many mysterious body conditions are caused by endocrine imbalance and it is unfortunately true that the medical profession remains mystified as to how to treat a number of these imbalances. There has been, in fact, a sad turning away from endocrinology by many doctors disappointed in the therapeutic value of working with the endocrines. We know that vitality depends upon sound activity of the endocrine glands, for they discharge powerful hormones and act as a stimulus to living cells. Thus, if a patient's adrenal or thyroid glands are underactive, some medical men reason, all one has to do is to administer adrenal or thyroid extract. When the extracts fail to accomplish the hoped-for results, these physicians lose interest in endocrinology. Among the disillusioned physicians are those who apparently completely disregard the largest endocrine gland of all, the liver, failing to realize that many of the disturbances of the endocrine glands would clear up if an unhealthy liver were restored to normal.

As the science of endocrinology advanced, it was found that the endocrine glands were responsible for such abnormalities as giants, dwarfs, cretins (stunted, deformed, and mentally deficient individuals), myxedematous individuals (grossly deficient in thyroid function, with dry and wrinkled skin, edema, and general mental and physical weakness), agromegalics (characterized by gigantism, enlarged head, feet, etc.), and various obese types. Much was learned from studies of the effects of removal of certain endocrine glands from animals in the laboratory. Changes in growth and temperament resulting from overstimulation of the various endocrine glands were also revealed. Most important of all, it became possible to predict and understand the cause and progress of many diseases characterized by symptoms due to endocrinologically controlled avenues of vicarious elimination.

To aid in the diagnosis and treatment of disease, endocrinology has paved the way by classifying people into three basic body types: (1) adrenal, (2) thyroid, (3) pituitary. These three types of people have not only different types of bodies, but different ways in which their organs of vicarious elimination function. These three distinct body types have different sex drives and appetites, and unique food requirements.

The Adrenal Type

Most of the information concerning the characteristics of the adrenal type has resulted from four sources of study: patients suffering from Addison's disease, in which adrenal secretion is deficient; animals and human beings whose adrenal glands have been removed; the selective breeding of animals; and patients with adrenal tumors. Among the animals, through careful breeding to augment adrenal strength, the draft horse, the shorthorn bull, and the bulldog are examples which tend to confirm observations made of human subjects.

Physical examination of the typical adrenal type shows the following characteristics:

Hair: Of head—coarse and often curly; of body—coarse and thick, often characterized by a "hairy ape" appearance

Features: Coarse, large, and heavy

Eyes: Iris shows ample pigmentation, either dark blue, brown, or black; pupil small and reacts instantly

Forehead: Low, usually with a low hair line

Nose: Well-developed, with large nostrils

Lips: Full, with strong color and warmth, due to ample circulation

Teeth: Large, especially the canines; yellowish in color; extremely hard and resistant to caries, dental arches full and round, third molars usually erupt normally

Tongue: Thick, wide, and clean; papillae coarse and thick

Palate: Low-arched and wide

Skull: Wide across the temples, lower jaw heavy, solid, and often protruding

Ears: Lobe thick, large, and long

Skin:	Thick, dry, and warm
Neck:	Thick and short; the characteristic bull neck
Chest:	Broad and thick, containing large heart and lungs
Abdomen:	Wide, thick, and often protuberant
Genitals:	Large
Extremities:	Thick and short; fingers and toes stubby; nails short, thick, and with moons small or lacking

The physical energy of the adrenal type is seemingly inexhaustible, as is the response of the sympathetic nervous system, a result of perfect oxidation of phosphorus in the nerve tissue. Oxidation of carbon in the muscular system gives the adrenal type his great warmth. Thus, the temperature of his body is scarcely ever below 98.8° F., with hands and feet always pleasantly warm. As digestion and detoxication of food poisons depend greatly upon oxidation in the liver and intestines, it follows that the typical adrenal type, with his perfect oxidation, has thorough digestion. In fact, he may and often does boast that he can eat any and all kinds of food without discomfort. The exogenous uric acid products as well as the indoxyl compounds are completely detoxicated in his liver and do not accumulate in the blood, nor are they found in his urine.

The skeletal muscles are well developed and have splendid tone. Fatigue is practically unknown to the adrenal type. His muscular endurance is spectacular. And the perfect tone of the involuntary muscles is evidenced by complete and rapid peristalsis, resulting in several bowel evacuations daily. He can dine on the most impossible food combinations imaginable because his stomach muscles operate so well that some foods can be sidetracked for continued action while other foods are switched into the small intestine. This faculty has been corroborated by X-ray studies and by gastric lavage.

The quality of the blood is characteristic. A slight-to-marked polycythemia (more red cells than usual) occurs; leucopenia (abnormal white cell count on the low side) is never noted. The blood, which is of a rich, red color, clots quickly. Fatal hemorrhage seldom occurs. The immunity against bacterial invasion is spectacular. The red cell sedimentation rate is slower than the so-called normal; often there is no apparent settling of the red corpuscles during the first hour of the test.

A member of the adrenal-type group has a phlegmatic disposition. He is easygoing, jolly, slow to anger, never bothered with insomnia or with fear. Customarily, he has a wide circle of friends because he is warm-hearted and surrounded by an "aura" of kindly sympathy. Splendid circulation gives him warm, magnetic hands, hence success as a masseur and magnetic healer; as a result, if he is sufficiently motivated, he may end up as an "irregular" doctor or healer.

Since members of this group have great muscular strength and patience, with an IQ usually in the lower range, they make up the bulk of the peasant-worker class or the unskilled labor group.

The Thyroid Type

Physical examination of the thyroid type of individual shows the following characteristics:

Hair: Of head—fine and silky; of body (except on pubis and in axillae)—hardly noticeable because it is so fine and thinly distributed

Features: Delicate and finely molded; great beauty is the rule

Eyes: Large and often slightly prominent—the type called "soulful"

Teeth: Narrowly spaced, of moderate size; pearly white, soft and not resistant to caries; dental arches usually V-shaped rather than round; partially erupted or unerupted third molars

Tongue: Moderately thin and long, with fine papillae and sensitivity

Palate:	High; more V-shaped than arched
Neck:	Graceful, thin, and long
Chest:	Long and thin; heart usually smaller than so-called normal; exquisitely shaped breasts in female; nipples more sensitive than in adrenal types
Abdomen:	Long and usually thin
Genitals:	Medium in size; increased sensitivity makes up for lack of size
Extremities:	Finely moulded, graceful hands; beautiful fingers, shapely, neither stubby nor markedly elongated

The most remarkable characteristic of the thyroid individual is his high-strung and extremely sensitive nervous system. He is the classic "race horse" type (just as the adrenal person is the "draft horse" type): thin, wiry, restless, quick, always on the jump, always listening, watching, smelling, because all of the special senses of the thyroid person are highly developed. The heart beat is usually above 72, and the least shock to his nervous system will result in an accelerated pulse.

Accompanying cardiac acceleration is increased secretion from the salivary and intestinal glands, liver, kidneys, and sweat glands. The liver discharges sugar into the bloodstream more rapidly, and if the pancreatic function which maintains the concentration of blood sugar is weak, glycosuria (sugar in the urine) follows. Because of a high metabolic rate, the body is likely, literally, to burn up and lose weight.

The cerebration of the thyroid individual is most interesting. Usually several streams of thought actually whirl through his brain at once, making concentration most difficult. He is frequently fatigued, dissatisfied with his surroundings, home, friends, and work.

In the adrenal type, it was noted that the adrenals determine whether or not the fire (oxidation) shall burn. The thyroid gland says how fast the fire shall burn.

Female members of the thyroid group, especially when the

gland is overstimulated, find their menstral cycle shortened, sometimes from 28 to 14 days. Their period of gestation is also shortened, from 280 days to 270 days or less. Generally, their babies are small and thin but usually healthy. The thyroid regulates the flow of breast milk, and it is the thin, wiry body types that have breast milk to spare.

Typically, the thyroid type suffers from insomnia and restlessness; when he finally does fall asleep, he dreams a great deal, with nightmares prevailing. Still, thyroid types awaken early, apparently fresh and with the day's plans formulated. Their sexual sensations are exquisitely developed. Orgasms, rapidly induced and frequently repeated, are accompanied with great intensity of feeling.

The Pituitary Type

Head:
: Large, skull high and often dome-like; frontal bone and superior orbital ridges often prominent

Features:
: Upper lip usually longer than normal

Teeth:
: Usually large, especially the central incisors

Joints:
: Laxity of all joints; knock-knees and flat feet are common

Extremities:
: Legs and arms long, which gives the tallness so commonly found in this type of person; fingers long and thin, with large moons on the nails

The chart of the pituitary type is less complete than that of the other two types because research is limited at present. Although it is more difficult to discuss the pituitary type of individual because conclusions, to date, are based mostly upon hypotheses, it is fairly agreed by the medical profession that oversecretion of the anterior pituitary may cause giants or acromegalics and that lack of this same secretion may result in dwarfism. An estimated ten thousand individuals in the United States are considered dwarfs because they lack this essential growth hormone.

There is also an understanding of how the enlarged anterior pituitary can press against the side walls of the sella turcica at the base of the skull, causing various degrees and kinds of headaches, and how the pressure can be exerted toward the optic chiasm (the crossing of the optic nerves just behind the eyeballs), resulting in diminution of the visual fields and perhaps total blindness. There is even weighty evidence that sudden swelling of an anterior pituitary gland restricted by a less roomy, rickets-deformed sella turcica can result in convulsions characteristic of epilepsy. But of the true effect of the anterior pituitary on what may be termed the higher brain functions, little is known. It is believed that the pituitary type is richer in "soul qualities"—intuition, creative ability, poetic expression, artistic temperament—and that his sexual drive is strongly developed.

As the reader attempts to fit himself into any of the above types, he will probably find that he does not wholly belong in any one category; he spills over. As Dr. Sheldon pointed out, the individual will always defy the statistics. Most of us are a combination of the three basic classic gland types. But one type is always dominant, and that one is the key to our physical and mental profiles. We are all aware that we belong either to the "morning people" who arise ready to conquer the world or to the "night people" who come alive late in the day; and we know that these varying metabolic patterns play havoc in marital relations—if we let them. Using the clues to personality and physique under discussion, we can do some important detective work on ourselves. "Know thyself" has ever been the philosopher's first maxim.

Since the so-called well-rounded individual cannot be strictly classified under any one of the glandular types, there is a method for determining which of the glands is truly dominant. For example, if the number 100 is taken for the normal value of any gland, then the normal person's pituitary, adrenals, and thyroid all would be 100. His glandular equation would be:

Pituitary 100; Thyroid 100; Adrenals 100

But the pituitary type would always be deficient in either thyroid or adrenals and thus might have an equation such as:

Pituitary 150; Thyroid 50; Adrenals 100

This equation might well represent the lazy, impractical dreamer. But if we find:

Pituitary 150; Thyroid 100; Adrenals 50

we might have the individual known as a genius. Because of the highly gifted individual's subnormal adrenals, it is often necessary for him to be constantly stimulating them. This he may do by excessive use of food stimulants such as meat, coffee, tea, and salt, or he may resort to alcohol, perhaps to narcotic drugs. When he lashes his adrenals to 100 percent activity, his pituitary and thyroid become overstimulated so that his equation reads:

Pituitary 200; Thyroid 150; Adrenals 100

In this state he has the most intense desire to work and to create. Following the period of overstimulation comes the inevitable depression, during which time he is unable to create anything at all—truly a suicidal state. If these periods of depression did not occur and the flames of artistic creation were kept blazing, sooner or later the adrenals would become entirely worn out, with a shortened life often resulting.

Sometimes, in all three body types, the male and female sexual apparatus become the avenues of vicarious elimination, the prostate in the male and the uterus in the female.

The basic plan of the sex apparatus in male and female is the same, and this correspondence is retained even after full sexual development. To express it mathematically, they are equal quantities with reversed signs. The male sex apparatus is the positive mold and the female apparatus the negative of the same basic pattern. They correspond like lock and key. The sex glands are similar in shape and size. They are known as testicles in man and ovaries in a woman. The male sex cells are called sperms; those of the female, eggs. Two ducts which originate near the sex glands transport the cells to the outside; they are known as seminal ducts in the male and as oviducts in the female. They meet in the midline of the body, forming a hollow organ. This organ is called the prostate in man and the uterus (womb) in the female. In the woman the duct becomes wide and the walls thin, in a body part that is therefore called the vagina (or sheath). In the man the duct remains narrow and the walls become thick, thus producing the penis.

Those parts of the sex apparatus which can be seen externally are called the external genitals. Despite the fact that they appear so different in man and woman, the external genitals are not fundamentally different but, as we have just indicated, are only differentiated terminal forms of one and the same basic pattern. During the first weeks of gestation one cannot tell outwardly, even when the genitals have already appeared, whether a human fetus will become a boy or a girl. In both cases one observes the same basic form: above, a tubercule; beneath it, a cleft; laterally, two swellings. The male genitals develop by the tubercule becoming large and thick, forming the penis and the cleft closing almost completely, leaving only the tiny opening for the urethra. Later, the testicles wander into the lateral folds and in doing so stretch them so that the folds become the scrotum. In a girl the tubercule remains small, becoming the clitoris; the cleft remains open, forming the vagina, and the folds become the labia.

During the last weeks of embryonic development the male sex glands leave the abdominal cavity through the inguinal rings and are suspended in a skin sac, the scrotum. The testicles are the only visceral organs that leave the abdominal cavity and exist outside it throughout life.

Each testicle contains about a thousand seminiferous tubules; the initial portion of each tubule is closed to make a kind of sac. The total length of the seminiferous tubules in both human testicles is a mile and a quarter. As a result of the constant production of cells, the mature sperm cells are slowly pushed forward through the seminiferous tubule and finally out of the testicle into the epididymis. The epididymis, the reservoir for sperm cells, is also a masterpiece of packing technique. Here a tube five yards long is folded until it is only two inches in length. For a sperm cell, which is one of the smallest cells in the body, five yards is a tremendous distance—proportionately as far as 120 miles would be for a full-grown man. The sperm cell is pushed forward along this entire distance.

From the epididymis the sperms are pushed into a tube, the seminal duct, which conducts them up into the abdominal cavity. Having reached the abdominal cavity, the two seminal ducts unite at the base of the bladder and enter the urethra. Up to this point the spermatic mass, or semen, is a dry crumbly substance, somewhat like the powder used to make puddings. Now it comes into contact with the fluids of the seminal vesicle and the prostate.

The seminal vesicles produce a yellowish fluid containing gelatinous globules. The product of the prostate is a milky secretion. When the male isn't toxic, it has a bland odor and a pleasant slightly sweet taste. When the prostate is being used as an avenue of vicarious elimination, the odor can resemble dead fish, and the taste may be either bitter or salty. Toxic secretions can be so acid they can cause blisters on the head of the penis, or when an orgasm deposits semen in the vagina, the woman may suffer from a burning, itching reaction, as a result of the acidic fluid implanted in her vagina.

Many of my female patients have complained of suffering pain, or a burning, itching sensation, directly after intercourse. Sometimes this acid secretion in either the male or female is mistaken for venereal disease and treated as such, to no avail.

The prostate contains not only glands but also muscle fibers, which surround the beginning of the urethra like the open end of a gas pipe, so that the urethra cannot be squeezed or torn by the filling of the bladder or the swelling of the penis. At the same time, muscle fibers form a valve mechanism which shuts off the urinary bladder so that the seminal fluid will not come into contact with the urine; the acid in the urine can damage the sperm cells. When the male is sexually excited, the muscle fibers of the prostate contract, closing off the urinary bladder. Not until sexual excitement has subsided does the muscle relax; the male is then able to urinate.

When in the male the prostate is affected, one of the chief irritants is salt. The organ itself is a walnut-size structure that sits astride the urethra at the entrance to the bladder. This strategic position is perfectly suited to its function of adding a powerful secretion to the seminal fluid at the moment of ejaculation, which increases the activity of the sperm.

If the male is extremely toxic and his liver and kidneys can no longer handle the overload of toxins, the prostate is sometimes used as an avenue of vicarious elimination. After the age of 40, more than 50 percent of all men suffer from enlargement of the prostate. As it enlarges, it progressively blocks the urethra and neck of the bladder. Ultimately, if the obstruction becomes complete, free urination is impossible.

Sexual complications arise when the gland is engorged prior to intercourse and sudden bladder obstruction ensues. A man in his fifties, or later, who through previous experience knows that sexual intercourse will make it impossible for him to pass his urine for the next eight to ten hours, will think twice about sex. Since the prostate enlarges in all directions simultaneously, other sexual structures feel the pressure and overall sexual performance declines.

A classic example of prostate problems was a 60-year-old patient from New York. His wife had died, and he had recently found companionship with an attractive divorcee. When it came to having intercourse, his prostate was so enlarged and painful he couldn't respond to his natural instincts. His urine test revealed a high percentage of salt. Close examination revealed a swollen liver and kidney malfunction. Immediately, I took him off salt. He admitted he salted everything until it was so whitened he could barely recognize the food underneath. I put him on a highly alkaline diet. It was almost three months before he showed any improvement.

In six months his prostate was back to normal. A year later he sent me a postcard from Europe. He was on his honeymoon.

Swelling of the prostate, difficulty in urination, pain during intercourse, inability to get or maintain an erection— all can be the result of salt, protein, sugar, or starch poisoning.

One of my patients, an engineer, was not able to maintain an erection. He had no previous history of sex problems and became very emotionally disturbed by his inability to complete the sex act. His urinalysis showed a heavy concentration of salt crystals. He was highly receptive to the food therapy plan I prescribed for him. Table salt and all salty foods were removed from his menu. In nine months his liver, kidneys, and prostate were performing normally; his potency was fully restored.

Another part of the male sexual apparatus is the urethra, a long, delicate tube which passes through the penis the length of its long axis. Since the penis stretches during sexual excitement, the urethra is not smooth like a rubber tube but is folded like the bellows of a camera. The wall of the urethra contains many mucous glands, of which two particularly large ones, Cowper's glands, lie directly in front of the prostate. During sexual excitement these glands secrete an alkaline mucus which neutralizes the traces of urine remaining in the urethral folds, thus creating an acid-free path for the sperm cells.

The penis is a cylinder, covered with skin, about as long as a finger. When at rest it is pendulous and flaccid. Because of its appearance, the tip of the penis is known as the glans, which means "acorn" in Latin; it is separated from the penile shaft by a groove. The inner surface of the foreskin covering the glans contains sebaceous glands, which create a sebaceous matter, the smegma. This secretion, when normal, contains odorous substances which attract the female during the act of love. If they are toxic, they can just as easily repel her.

If the man is to complete the sex act with the female, he must be able to attain an erection. Erections occur as the result of sexual stimulation; the penis fills with blood. The normal blood pressure would not be sufficient for the erection of the penis, so that this swelling in size, tension, and position is carried out by means of an interesting and complex mechanism.

The interior of the penis, the space between the urethra in the central axis and the cutaneous wall of the penis, is filled with three cigar-shaped chambers, the corpora cavernosa, which can be compared with the gas chambers of a dirigible. The corpus cavernosum consists of connective tissue chambers, the walls of which contain numerous blood vessels. When at rest they are contracted and permit only traces of blood to pass through, so that the chambers remain empty.

Under the influence of sexual excitement, the contracted vessels relax and the blood flows without hindrance into the vessels and then through and into the chambers of the corpora cavernosa. Owing to the expansion of the chambers of the connective tissue, "guy ropes" of the urethra are tautened in all directions so that the urethra itself expands without being compressed by the pressure of the blood. To obtain a state of increased pressure within the penis the outflow veins are closed during an erection. These veins originate in especially thin-walled peripheral chambers which are open when the organ is at rest and which supply the tissues with nutriment. During erection, however, they are compressed by the pressure of the blood.

As sexual excitement subsides, the vessels begin to contract again, the blood leaves the penis slowly through the funnel veins, and finally, when the pressure against the peripheral veins has relaxed, it flows very rapidly through the large dorsal vein.

The semen is expelled by a series of spasmodic contractions of the urethra. The filling of the testicle with semen creates a feeling of tension; the expulsion of the sperm gives rise to a feeling of relaxation mingled with strong sensations of pleasure—that is, if the man is in good health and his secretions are normal.

When the body's natural energy flow is off balance because of the necessity of eliminating heavy toxic loads through the natural eliminative organs and the vicarious organs of elimination, there is little or no energy left to obtain or maintain an erection, leaving the male impotent. Like all bodily activities and movements, the erection of the penis and the ejaculation of the semen take place under control of the nervous system. In the lumbar region, approximately at the level where a belt crosses the lower back, the spinal cord contains a nerve center whose motor cells stimulate the dilation of the corpora cavernosa and the expulsion of the semen by wave-like contractions of the urethra. This is referred to as the erection center. This center is under control of the cerebral cortex, which in turn is stimulated by sensory impressions and by the imagination, as well as by hormones. The erection of the penis is the result of the cooperation of a large number of widely separated, independent organs. The body of the male must be functioning normally to fully enjoy the sex act.

The female's organs are the ovaries and the oviducts, or tubes, which unite in the midline with the uterus. The latter opens into the vagina, which in turn communicates with the surface of the body. Here are to be found the external genitals: the clitoris, the labia minora and majora, and the vaginal entrance, half-closed by the hymen. Parallel to the sex canal is the urinary canal, consisting of the bladder, the urethra, and the urethral orifice.

The external genitals are the two lateral swellings, which correspond to the male scrotum, developed as two pairs of skin folds, the (outer) labia majora and the (inner) labia minora. The folds of the labia minora contain two glands corresponding to Cowper's glands in the male; these are

Bartholin's glands. During sexual excitement they produce a mucus that wells forth between the labia and makes it easier for a man, whose glans is also covered with mucus, to insert his penis smoothly into the vagina.

The urethra is situated in the anterior upper angle between the labia minora. Above and in front of the urethral orifice, covered by the folds of the labia and withdrawn when not in a state of erection, lies the clitoris. The clitoris corresponds to the male penis and, like the penis, it is filled with cavernous tissue that swells during sexual excitement, enabling it to emerge from its hiding place. Similarly, the vaginal entrance is padded with cavernous tissue that swells during sexual excitement, thus narrowing the vaginal entrance.

The vagina is a tube lined with mucous membrane, approximately two and a half inches long, extending from the vaginal entrance to the entrance of the womb. The wall of the vagina continually sheds cells that contain glycogen. By means of an enzyme the glycogen is broken down to glucose, a sugar that serves as a nutritive medium for bacteria. Bacterial activity leads to the formation of lactic acid so that the vagina, like the stomach, contains an acid secretion. The lactic acid bacilli of the vagina, like those of the stomach, form a bacterial flora that hinders the growth of other bacilli and prevents pathogenic organisms of the external world from ascending to the upper sections of the sex canal. The bacterial flora of the vagina is a woman's best protection against infection. For this reason habitual vaginal douches, especially with disinfecting agents, are to be rejected as unnatural.

The lactic acid of the vagina is also of great importance for fertilization. Sperm cells are damaged by acids and consequently flee from an acid milieu. If a piece of vaginal mucous membrane is placed among living sperm cells, the latter soon retreat from the membrane, leaving it isolated. Alkaline mucus drips from the uterus into the vagina and attracts the sperm cells. After the sperm cells have been deposited by ejaculation in the posterior portion of the vagina, they flee from the acid vagina to the uterus, to which they are attracted by the alkaline mucus.

The uterus or womb is a hollow, pear-shaped organ consisting chiefly of muscle fibers and lined with a mucous membrane containing many mucous glands. The broad massive portion is called the body; the narrow part is the neck. The uterus, which is hollow, is suspended in the female pelvis with the neck downward. If a pear is cut open and the core removed one has a complete model of the uterus.

Great damage is done to the womb when it is forced into the service of vicarious elimination. Inflammation may be caused by white sugar and white sugar products, and red, irritating areas in the womb, thereby causing cramps in between menstral periods or an aching feeling in the lower back.

A pleasant, slightly sweet secretion is what is supposed to lubricate the vagina in preparation for intercourse. When the womb is inflammed, an acid secretion with a putrid smell and salty taste burns the vaginal walls, as well as the male's penis, during the act of intercourse. The vagina additionally produces a yellowish, pasty discharge called leukorrhea, which also has an odor. Needless to say, such abnormal conditions leave the genital tract open to infection; many hysterectomies, performed because of an infected womb, are really unnecessary. Treating the infection should have been considered first.

What is the solution to such problems? The solution is simply to restore liver and kidney function and to eliminate the burden of vicarious elimination from the womb.

Many times the patient can be saved by bed rest and food therapy. And by education that leads to a complete change from destructive habit patterns to constructive ones.

To summarize: In the pituitary type of individual, the main avenue of vicarious elimination is the pituitary gland. (The pituitary type is more prone to migraine headaches than the other types.) The thyroid type eliminates through the inner and outer and middle skin. The adrenal type eliminates through the lymphatic glands in the body.

All three types eliminate through the uterus (womb) and prostate gland.

Disease, as I see it, is an unnatural elimination process. To facilitate the natural elimination of toxic material and return the patient to sexual health, I prescribe an individual diet to have the patient abstain from the dead foods and toxic substances that created the toxemia in the first place.

Body Types and Sexual Appetites

Each body type, the adrenal, the thyroid, and the pituitary, has a different sexual appetite and a different attitude toward sex. Although no two human beings are exactly alike, and are usually classified into the three basic endocrine groups noted above, it must be remembered also that any individual of any type can be either toxic or non-toxic depending upon previous diet.

The sexually healthy adrenal type, male or female, is generally a very easy person to live with, as his temperament is level and easygoing and his disposition is naturally happy. He is warm, kind, patient, muscularly strong, a good sleeper, and a good worker. He has excellent digestion and elimination and is hardly ever sick. If his thyroid and pituitary glands are relatively inactive, his life and his happiness consists of eating and sleeping. He comes home from work, eats dinner, after which he views television and usually falls asleep. If he has had a hard day, it is likely he will not be easily aroused sexually. If he does have sex, he enjoys it and, as a rule, immediately falls into a post-orgasmic sleep. His sex drives are more on an animal-instinct level, with male and female both exhibiting great endurance during the sex act.

The sexually unhealthy adrenal type shows irritations from chemical stimulants and depressants due to his past dietary life. Salt excess can make him aggressively sexual. Alcohol also greatly stimulates him, often sexually, and it matters little whether he drinks it or creates it in his digestive tract as the result of a highly fermentable diet. Though he tends to be lazy, he can be so irritated by salt and defective liver function that his temper is uncontrollable. During late middle age, this type is prone to develop arteriosclerosis and maybe have a heart attack. At early middle age he sometimes becomes impotent, usually as a result of relatively poor thyroid and pituitary glands.

The sexually healthy thyroid types have the greatest feeling and pleasure in sexual relations. They are high-strung, nervous, acutely aware of pleasure and pain. Their hearts beat more rapidly than the adrenal type, their reactions are quick, and they are able to have violent and frequent orgasms. As they feel more deeply, they love more deeply and are the happiest people in their sex life. These individuals are usually the thin, racehorse type of people, with rapid cerebration.

The sexually unhealthy thyroid types are most miserable. Excess salt, sugar, and starch in their diet can result in grave complications. When their liver function becomes impaired from improper diet, a vicarious elimination of toxins takes place through their skins. If the outside skin is called into play a whole series of ugly skin diseases appear. If the inside skin or mucous membrane is involved, mucous inflammation results, causing the commonly called "catarrhal diseases" which can involve mucous membranes anywhere in the body. If the middle skin is involved, arthritis usually results.

In the woman, excess sugar and salt (when the liver is defective a very small amount of sugar and salt may be an excess) can irritate and inflame the womb and can cause a whole series of gynecological disturbances, such as painful menstruation, flooding, enlarged and boggy uterus, and finally fibroid tumors.

In the man, the prostate can be inflamed, especially from salt and sweet foods. Mental irritability, fatigue, premature ejaculation, frequent or painful or spasmodic urination, can result. Finally, there ensue prostate fibroid tumors or a large boggy prostate, either condition frequently requiring surgery.

The sexually healthy pituitary type enjoys sex to the utmost. The pituitary gland, which lies at the base of the brain, is directly connected by nerves to the large sex centers in the frontal lobes of the brain. The pituitary is most important as far as sex is concerned, for without its secretion there can be no sex. The pituitary person, especially if he is healthy, which usually means he has a good thyroid, can enjoy to the greatest extent the idealisms and dreams and mental stimulation of sex.

The sexually unhealthy pituitary type can be so violently overstimulated by improper diet that his sex life is uncontrollable. These are the men who rape women and attack little children, the women who become nymphomaniacs, the people who literally exhaust themselves sexually. As they grow weaker and weaker from sex-exhausted adrenals (which are often weak in the first place), they become more and more miserable and frequently die at an early age.

Food Needs of Each Body Type

Just as each body type has a different sexual appetite, each endocrine body type has some unique set of individual requirements.

The adrenal type of person, for instance, when healthy, has a digestive system superior to those of the other two types. When young and in good health, he has been known to eat some toxic combinations that would adversely affect the thyroid or pituitary type. Yet he has been able to digest these toxic combinations without ill effect.

The adrenal type has such good elimination that if he does eat poisoned food, by chance, or toxic combinations, he may often eliminate them immediately by either vomiting or diarrhea. By nature, such people have a lot of drive and energy; they need considerable physical activity, like walking, swimming, sports, especially when young, and a regular sexual relationship.

Their diet should be well balanced, with proteins, large amounts of vegetables, raw and cooked, plenty of fresh fruit, and small amounts of starch. They need more meat than the other types.

Adrenal type children should be taught not to indulge in rich desserts and heavy starches, for they usually love to eat and it is easy for them to put on weight. If they are ill, they frequently will swell with water, since they have a large lymphatic tree. Poison is stored by the adrenal types, when toxic, in their lymphatic tree until they are well enough to pass it out through the natural eliminative organs.

The thyroid person is very sensitive. His rate of metabolism is usually higher than those of the adrenal and pituitary types. He needs more rest than the adrenal or pituitary person and requires more protein because his thyroid works faster and he burns food more rapidly. The thyroid type also needs more calcium than the adrenal. The thyroid male or female must be very careful not to overindulge in sodium chloride (table salt) because too much salt causes the iodine in the thyroid to be replaced with chlorine; then thyroid problems may arise.

It is better for the thyroid type to eat five or six small meals a day than to overeat at any one meal, because his digestive system is not as strong as that of his adrenal brothers or sisters.

The thyroid individual must be careful to stay away from emotionally upsetting people and situations. Emotional upsets affect his metabolism, digestion and eliminative systems more easily than those of the easygoing adrenal type, often making him suffer psychosomatic illness that causes physical illness. Creative hobbies that he or she may enjoy are helpful to this particular type of person, because he often needs quiet periods by himself.

The thyroid person must learn how much and what kind of food is best for him to maintain vibrant health. He may do this by experimenting with the optimum food list (see Chapter 21). He must also determine how much sex activity is best for his particular physiological and psychological needs.

The pituitary type, normally with a superior mind and having a strong sex drive, often finds it difficult to stay true to one person. Many of them can have sex with two or more partners in a single day.

Salt, coffee, and alcohol toxemias can create problems in the sex center of the brain and cause overindulgence in sexual activities, resulting in a severe depletion of the adrenals. As a rule, toxins attack the brain sex center more readily in the pituitary type than in the adrenal or thyroid.

Pituitary people should build their diets on large amounts of raw and cooked vegetables and fresh fruits, along with proteins; starches and sugars should be kept to a minimum.

DEAD FOOD – A KEY TO SEXUAL MALFUNCTION 9

What is a habit pattern?

Simply a pattern of action that is acquired and has become so automatic that it is difficult to break. An acquired habit, from the physiological point of view, is a new pathway of discharge formed in the brain, by which certain incoming currents ever after tend to escape.

Driving a car is a good example. At first, we are conscious of every move we make, each act seems mechanical; we *know* we're at the wheel. We have to consciously remember to switch on the ignition to start the motor, when to apply foot to brake, when to signal. Driving, like any other new set of habit patterns, can be confusing. However, in less than a year, we drive almost automatically.

Eating is a habit pattern, formed early in childhood. At first we are fed our parents' favorite foods, subconsciously influenced by their attitudes about what they choose to eat.

I remember a patient of mine whose year-and-a-half-old baby boy had enjoyed liver until the patient's sister began to take care of him. Once a week, my patient went to play bridge. The baby was fed liver and vegetables by the aunt who, it turned out, hated liver and made faces while feeding him. Within a period of a month the child began to make faces and then refused to eat liver anymore.

Eating becomes, at an early age, a conditioned way of life that helps bolster emotional security. Food becomes a reward or a punishment, as the case may be. Overindulgence, so frequently considered a reward, all too often proves to be a self-punishment.

I remember when I first graduated from medical school, I thought chocolate-covered marshmallow cookies were the most satisfying food in the world; also, chocolate ice cream was the next best thing to heaven. I promised myself that as soon as I began making money I would reward myself with these pleasure-filled foods. And I did just that. For years, I ate at least one box of cookies a day, as well as a daily quart of chocolate ice cream.

Once the body becomes toxic, it seems that the desire for stimulation from toxic food increases. In my case, the more I consumed the more I craved. Soon I became addicted to sweet pastries, and eventually acquired the habit of licking salt which I poured into the palm of my hand. All my food was doused in salt.

Before long, I was leaning heavily on the false stimulation of the salt, chocolate, and sweet starches. My practice had increased and I was working long hours. In time, I began to suffer attacks of asthma.

When my health broke down, I was forced to see how my own overindulgence had robbed me of a healthy, normally functioning body. I began to see the correlation between pure food and health, and also between toxin-producing food and drink with ill-health, cellular impairment and breakdown, which are sometimes followed by early death.

In 1922, as the result of careful diet, I was able to effect a cure for my asthma. Shortly thereafter I discarded the tenets of orthodox medicine in favor of the dietary approach.

I was soon to put this new approach to healing to its first test. A farmer's wife came to my office with a fibroid tumor, about the size of a large egg, located above her collarbone. It had been operated upon with no success because it was so deeply buried in the nerves and blood vessels.

Upon examination of her urine, I found a tremendous excess of sulfur protein. I learned, by questioning her, that she and her husband owned a turkey ranch and that before the tumor developed she had been eating turkey three times a day for a good many months because they had been unable to sell their fowl.

As a first step in her treatment I suggested removal of all sulfur from her diet and an increase of alkaline intake through the addition of vegetables and fruits. She immediately omitted the sulfur-rich vegetables of the cabbage family and others and, of course, animal and seafood proteins, including turkeys, which are also rich in sulfur.

After she had been six months on this rigid sulfur-free diet, the tumor had shrunk to half its size. And after one year it disappeared entirely.

The patient remained on an animal-protein-free diet for two years, then she added rare beef or lamb and a small amount of milk while continuing with generous helpings of all the sulfur-free vegetables and fruits. I realized from this experience, and my earlier one with asthma, the importance of dietary temperance and moderation.

My understanding of the role of temperance in the healing process was further reinforced by an important book given to me by one of my patients. The material in the book, *The Art of Living Long,* published by William F. Butler in Milwaukee, Wisconsin, in 1903, a new and improved English version of an earlier original, was an excellent teacher.

The author of the book, Luigi Cornaro, was a celebrated Venetian centenarian, who was born in 1464 and died in 1566 at the age of 102 years. The average life expectancy at that time was 31. Cornaro outlived all of his contemporaries.

His book, *Discorsi della Vita Sobria* (original volume), literally *Discourses on the Moderate Life,* was published in 1558, at age 94. The book was well known in his time and for a century or more afterward. Joseph Addison, writing in the *Spectator* (October 3, 1711; Number 195) early in the eighteenth century, said:

> ... the most remarkable instance of the efficacy of temperance toward the procuring of long life is what we meet with in a little book published by Luigi Cornaro the Venetian; which I mention because it is of undoubted credit, as the late Venetian ambassador, who was of the same family, attested more than once in conversation, when he resided in England. Cornaro, who was the author of the little treatise I am mentioning, was of an infirm constitution, until about forty, when by obstinately persisting in an exact course of temperance, he recovered a perfect state of health; insomuch that at four score he published his book, which has been translated into English under the title of "Sure and Certain Methods of Attaining a Long and Healthy Life." He lived to give a third or fourth edition of it; and after having passed his hundredth year, died without pain or agony, and like one who falls asleep. The treatise I mention has been taken notice of by several eminent authors, and is written with such a spirit of cheerfulness, religion, and good sense, as are the natural concomitants of temperance and sobriety. The mixture of the old man in it is rather a recommendation than a discredit to it.

Part of Luigi Cornaro's philosophy is stated in the words of the Roman emperor and philosopher, Marcus Aurelius Antoninus:

> If any man can convince me and bring home to me that I do not think as I act aright, gladly will I change; for I search after truth, by which man never yet was harmed. But he is harmed who abideth on still in his deception and ignorance.
>
> Do not think what is hard for thee to master is impossible for man; but if a thing is possible and proper to man, deem it attainable by thee.
>
> Persevere then until thou shalt have made these things thy own.

In order to accomplish the purpose uppermost in his mind, the first thing to which Cornaro gave his constant and most intelligent attention was the securing of perfect health, which hitherto he had never known.

Luigi Cornaro was born with a very delicate constitution, accompanied unfortunately by a choleric disposition. He furthermore gave evidence in early life of careless habits, which finally developed into those of intemperance. He had almost destroyed himself by the time he reached the age of 40. Finally convinced that his unnatural habits would be the cause of his death he decided, with singleness of purpose, to change.

The autobiography of Cornaro shows that, after patient search, he discovered in his own person the curative and life-sustaining power of the temperate life. He pictures the reward to be reaped every moment, but especially in old age, from a life spent in conformity with reason and Nature. He stated, "I never knew the world was beautiful until I reached old age."

Most particularly does he emphasize the greater value of the later years of life compared with the earlier ones. By the time men have acquired knowledge, judgement, and experience—the necessary equipment for the fullest citizenship—they are unable, he observes, because of physical degeneration, due to irrational and unnatural methods of living, to exercise these qualifications. Such men are then cut off in their prime, leaving at 40, 50 or 60 their lifework but half completed.

Cornaro began his book at 83. He states: "It is certain that habit, in man, eventually becomes second nature compelling him to practice that to which he has become accustomed, regardless of whether such a thing be beneficial, or injurious to him. Moreover, we see in many instances—and no one can call this into question—that the force of habit will triumph, even over reason.

"It is in consequence of this powerful force of habit, that of late,—indeed during my own lifetime and memory,—three evil customs have gradually gained a foothold in our own Italy. The first of these is adulation and ceremony, the second is heresy, and the third is intemperance. These three vices, cruel monsters of human life as they truly are, have, in our day, prevailed so universally as to have impaired the sincerity of social life, the religion of the soul, and the health of the body.

"Having long reflected on this unfortunate condition, I have now determined to treat of the last of these vices—intemperance; and, in order to accomplish all I can toward abolishing it, I shall prove that it is an abuse. With regard to the two other obnoxious habits, I feel certain that, ere long, some noble mind will undertake the task of condemning them and removing them from among us. Thus do I firmly hope that I shall, before I leave this world, see these three abuses conquered and crushed out of Italy, and, consequently, witness the return of my country to her wise and beautiful customs of yore.

"Coming, then, to that evil concerning which I propose to speak,—the vice of intemperance,—I declare that it is a wicked thing that it should prevail to such an extent as to greatly lower, nay, almost abolish, the temperate life. For though it is well known that intemperance proceeds from the vice of gluttony, and temperance from the virtue of restraint, nevertheless the former is exalted as a virtuous thing and even as a mark of distinction, while temperance is stigmatized and scorned as dishonorable, and as befitting the miserly alone.

"These false notions are due entirely to the force of habit, bred by men's senses and uncontrolled appetites. It is this craving to gratify the appetites which has allured and inebriated men to such a degree that, abandoning the path of virtue, they have taken to following the one of vice—a road which leads them, though they see it not, to strange and fatal chronic infirmities through which they grow prematurely old. Before they reach the age of forty their health has been completely worn out—just the reverse of what the temtemperate life once did for them. For this, before it was banished by the deadly habit of intemperance, invariably kept all its followers strong and healthy, even to the age of fourscore and upward.

"O wretched and unhappy Italy, canst thou not see that intemperance kills every year amongst thy people as great a number as would perish during the time of a most dreadful pestilence, or by the sword or fire of many bloody wars! And these truly immoral banquets of thine, now so commonly the custom,—feasts so great and intolerable that the tables are never found large enough to accommodate the innumerable dishes set upon them, so that they must be heaped, one upon another, almost mountain high,—must we not brand them as so many destructive battles! Who could ever live amid such a multitude of disorders and excesses!

"For there is a remedy by which we may banish this fatal vice of intemperance—an easy remedy, and one of which every man may avail himself if he will; that is, to live in accordance with the simplicity of Nature, which teaches us to be satisfied with little, to follow the ways of holy self-control and divine reason, and to accustom ourselves to eat nothing but that which is necessary to sustain life.

"We should bear in mind that anything more than this will surely be followed by infirmity and death; and that while intemperance is merely a gratification of the palate,—a pleasure that vanishes in a moment,—yet, for a long time afterward, it causes the body much suffering and damage, and finally destroys it together with the soul.

"The excesses of my past life, together with my bad constitution,—my stomach being very cold and moist,—had caused me to fall a prey to various ailments, such as pains in the stomach, frequent pains in the side, symptoms of gout, and, still worse, a low fever that was almost continuous; but I suffered especially from disorder of the stomach, and from an unquenchable thirst. This evil—nay, worse than evil—condition left me nothing to hope for myself, except that death should terminate my troubles and the weariness of my life—a life as yet far removed from its natural end, though brought near to a close by my wrong manner of living.

"After every known means of cure had been tried, without affording me any relief, I was, between my thirty-fifth and fortieth years, reduced to so infirm a condition that my physicians declared there was but one remedy left for my ills —a remedy which would surely conquer them, provided I would make up my mind to apply it and persevere patiently in its use.

"That remedy was the temperate and orderly life, . . . My physicians warned me that if I neglected to apply this remedy, in a short time it would be too late to derive any benefit from it; for, in a few months, I should surely die.

"Having been instructed by my physicians as to the method I was to adopt, I understood that I was not to partake of any foods, either solid or liquid, save such as are prescribed for invalids; and, of these, in small quantities only. To tell the truth, diet had been prescribed for me before; but it had been at a time, when, preferring to live as I pleased and being weary of such foods, I did not refrain from gratifying myself by eating freely of all those things which were to my taste. And being consumed, as it were, by fever, I did not hesitate to continue drinking, and in large quantities, the wines which pleased my palate. Of all this, of course, after the fashion of invalids, I never breathed a word to my physicians.

"Within a few days I began to realize that this new life suited my health excellently; and, persevering in it, in less than a year—though the fact may seem incredible to some—I found myself entirely cured of all my complaints.

"Now that I was in perfect health, I began to consider seriously the power and virtue of order . . . Accordingly, I began to observe very diligently what kinds of food agree with me. I determined, in the first place, to experiment with those which were most agreeable to my palate, in order that I might learn if they were suited to my stomach and constitution. The proverb 'Whatever tastes good will nourish and strengthen,' is generally regarded as embodying a truth, and is invoked, as a first principle, by those who are sensually inclined. In it I had hitherto firmly believed; but now I was resolved to test the matter, and find to what extent, if any, it was true.

"My experience, however, proved this saying to be false. For instance, dry and very cold wine was agreeable to my taste; as were also melons; and, among other garden produce, raw salads; also fish, pork, tarts, vegetable soups, pastries, and

other similar articles. All of these, I say, suited my taste
exactly, and yet I found they were hurtful to me. Thus
having, by my own experience, proved the proverb in
question to be erroneous, I ever after looked upon it as such,
and gave up the use of that kind of food and of that kind of
wine, as well as cold drinking. Instead, I chose only such
wines as agreed with my stomach, taking of them only such a
quantity as I knew it could easily digest; and I observed the
same rule with regard to my food, exercising care both as to
the quantity and the quality. In this manner, I accustomed
myself to the habit of never fully satisfying my appetite,
either with eating or drinking—always leaving the table well
able to take more. In this I acted according to the proverb:
'Not to satiate one's self with food is the science of health.'

"Being thus rid, for the reasons and in the manner I have
given, of intemperance and disorder, I devoted myself
entirely to the sober and regular life. This had such beneficial
effect upon me that, in less than a year as I have just said, I
was entirely freed from all the ills which had been so deeply
rooted in my system as to have become almost incurable.

"Another excellent result which this new life effected in
me was that I no longer fell sick every year—as I had always
previously done following my former sensual manner of
life—with strange fever, which at times had brought me near
to death's door; but, under my new regimen, from this also
was I delivered.

"In a word, I grew most healthy; and I have remained so
from that time to this day, and for no other reason than that
of my constant fidelity to the orderly life. The unbounded
virtue of that is, that that which I eat and drink,—always
being such as agrees with my constitution and, in quantity,
such as it should be,—after it has imparted its invigorating
elements to my body, leaves it without any difficulty and
without ever generating within it any bad humors. Whence,
following this rule, as I have already said, I have constantly
been, and am now—thank God!—most healthy.

"It is true, however, that besides these two very important

rules which I have always so carefully observed, relative to eating and drinking,—namely, to take only the quantity which my stomach can easily digest and only the kinds that agree with it,—I have also been careful to guard against great heat and cold, as well as extreme fatigue or excesses of any nature; I have never allowed my accustomed sleep and rest to be interfered with; I have avoided remaining for any length of time in places poorly ventilated; and have been careful not to expose myself too much to the wind or the sun; for these things, too, are great disorders. Yet it is not a very difficult matter to avoid them; for, in a being endowed with reason, the desire of life and health possesses greater weight than the mere pleasure of doing things which are known to be hurtful.

"I have also preserved myself, as far as I have been able, from those other disorders from which it is more difficult to be exempt; I mean melancholy, hatred, and the other passions of the soul, which all appear greatly to affect the body. However, my efforts in this direction have not been so successful as to preserve me wholly; since, on more than one occasion, I have been subject to either one or the other of these disturbances, not to say all of them. Yet even this fact has proved useful to me; for my experience has convinced me that, in reality, these disorders have not much power over, nor can they do much harm to, the bodies of these whose lives are governed by the two rules I have already mentioned relative to eating and drinking. So I can say, with truth, that whosoever observes these two principal rules can suffer but little from any disorder.

"Galen, the famous physician, bore testimony to this truth long before my time. He asserts that all other disorders caused him but very little harm, because he had learned to guard against those of excessive eating and drinking; and that, for this reason, he was never indisposed for more than a day. Nature has taught me that she is satisfied with little; that my spare diet has been found sufficient to preserve me in health all these many years, and that, with me, this abstemious habit had long since become second nature. I maintained, furthermore, that it was in harmony with reason that, as my age increased, I should diminish, rather than increase, the quantity of my food."

Cornaro quoted this proverb: "The food from which a man abstains, after he has eaten heartily, is of more benefit to him than that which he has eaten."

"I have learned through experience, what is the best food for me. It is said, 'A man cannot be a perfect physician of anyone save himself alone.'

"Who would believe, for instance, that wine over a year old would be hurtful to my stomach, while new wine would be suitable to it? And that pepper, which is commonly considered a heating spice, would not act upon me as such, but that cinnamon would warm and help me?

"Let us be truthful. Men are, as a rule, very sensual and intemperate and wish to gratify their false appetites, no matter the cost.

"Furthermore, the aforesaid followers of overindulgence in sensuality will tell you that the temperate and orderly life is an impossible one. To which I answer Galen, great as a physician as he was, led it, and chose it as the best medicine. So likewise did Plato, Cicero, Isocrates and many other famous men in time past, choose to live the temperate life.

"Another answer to this objection—and a better one—is, that he who leads the temperate life can never fall sick, or at least can do so only rarely, and his indisposition lasts but a very short while. For by living temperately, he removes all causes of illnesses; and having removed these, he thereby removes the effects."

Luigi Cornaro's entire philosophy is based on temperance, small amounts of simple food, and not too much liquid. The discipline of learning new habit patterns and staying with them throughout life until they become automatic was one of Cornaro's finest lessons for me.

From one of my patients I learned how deeply destructive habit patterns can affect a life. He was a motion picture producer, a talented and creative man. He had recently remarried when I first met him.

The death sentence had already been passed on him by a heart specialist, who warned the producer's then prospective bride not to marry him. He was classified as a cardiac case with advanced arteriosclerosis who required thirty nitroglycerin tablets every twenty-four hours.

He came to me after he had recovered from his first "heart attack." My diagnosis showed that he was not a cardiac case at all, but that he had serious liver and kidney damage. I outlined a very simple diet and, within two months, his blood pressure dropped one hundred points. I felt he had a chance to live.

At this time my patient was living in Palm Springs. He was feeling much better, so he went to a restaurant and ate a salad with a very sharp salad dressing and a thick salt-laden pea soup with ham. He suffered a midnight attack, and was hospitalized.

I was on my annual summer vacation, and a local doctor put him back on nitroglycerin. It did not alleviate his extreme pain.

His wife remembered the zucchini soup formula I had prescribed: parsley, celery, zucchini. She began giving him the soup every hour and a half; within nine hours her husband needed no drugs whatever.

He began to feel very well and went to Tahiti. Then he returned to the old pattern of eating rich French food and his attacks returned. Again, his wife put him on the soup diet, but as soon as he felt better, he would immediately revert to his intemperate eating habits.

The last trip was to Hong Kong, a luxury cruise on a flagship. Four or five nights a week were spent in elaborate dinners and costume parties. During that time the patient was in sick bay more than he was out of it. He contracted pneumonia in Hong Kong. He was given penicillin. He woke up one morning, after his return home to America, his back a mass of bleeding sores. The eruption was diagnosed as a staphlycoccus infection. I was called in and prescribed zucchini soup. By the third day the infection had cleared.

I then sent the following letter to his wife:

I am going to describe your husband's condition more fully so that you can understand, and help more.

During the last four years his liver has gradually deteriorated, as have his once powerful adrenal glands. There was a time when it was possible to reduce his blood pressure and improve his liver, and build up his adrenals. At that time he had a margin of safety, and his controlled metabolism was adequate.

Now we have a different situation—the liver is poor, the adrenals are almost depleted, the thyroid is pinch-hitting for the liver and adrenals, but its overactivity is ruining the heart. His appetite and craving for foods is in his head. His digestion is nearly gone.

Your husband's attacks from food intoxication and drugs only stimulate what is left of the adrenals. But soon they will be exhausted. The dropsy in body and lungs is Nature's effort to sidetrack toxins, so as not to put too much load on the heart. I feel that his power of digestion and liver function are irreparably damaged, and his margin is gone, and that he is nearing adrenal depletion, which means the end.

Three times in the last month of his life he was rushed by ambulance to the intensive care unit of a nearby hospital; tourniquets were placed above his knees and his elbows to try to drain the dropsy, and clear the toxins out of his lungs and his body. The last time he was taken to the hospital, and put under morphine sedation, his blood pressure dropped steadily and he passed away.

An autopsy revealed massive liver and kidney damage as the main cause of death.

I felt a sense of sadness and loss when his wife called to tell me of his passing and to thank me for giving him four years of life she felt he wouldn't have had otherwise.

Another case from my files that almost ended tragically is one of a college student, a young woman, who was suffering from pernicious anemia, heart imbalance, a womb infection, and obesity. She was very short and small-boned and weighed close to two hundred pounds. This patient had the appearance of a pale, pasty-skinned sausage about ready to burst.

She had fallen in love with a professional man a few years her senior who wanted to marry her and was naturally concerned about the state of her health. He was afraid of the possibility of her having a heart attack, as she complained constantly of pains and palpitations in her heart, pain in the upper part of her back as well as in the area of her liver. Her condition precluded any sexual intercourse.

Her first examination, urinalysis, and diagnosis revealed serious liver damage and kidney malfunction. Because she was an adrenal type, poisons were being sidetracked into her lymph channels, which caused bloating as well as pressure on the heart. She also had an infection in her womb.

This patient's food history was a study in overindulgence. Before noon she would consume far too many cups of coffee, and usually ate sweet pastry for breakfast. For lunch, she ate white-bread sandwiches, had pie or ice cream for dessert, and more coffee. After classes, before dinnertime, she would have a few cocktails. Dinner consisted of heavy starches followed by dessert and more coffee.

Her compulsive eating habits were formed early in childhood. She was of German descent, and had been brought up on large quantities of food, especially breads, pies, cakes and pastries. As a consequence, her patterns of compulsive eating became intensified as she developed into womanhood. It was not unusual for her to get up at night and raid the refrigerator.

Finally, as a result of her continued intemperance, her liver and kidneys could no longer strain and filter out the toxic acids. Her avenues of vicarious elimination were depleted, particularly her endocrine glands, and one day she collapsed at college.

The collapse was diagnosed as a heart attack, but she had actually experienced a liver attack. I prescribed bed rest for a week, and allowed her only vegetable broth as food. Much of the congestion in her liver was thus eliminated.

She followed this food therapy for a period of three months. Then, as soon as she felt better, she went off the diet. She had another attack, then back again to her diet. This seesaw pattern continued until she finally suffered another serious attack at school and was hospitalized.

During her next visit we extensively discussed her habit patterns. I pointed out to her that an act becomes easier after being done several times. Simply, the only way to change a destructive habit pattern is to replace it with a constructive or positive one. This must be a conscious act of discipline on the part of the patient. And such a discipline is best supported by not hoping to conquer the problem all at once, but on a day-to-day basis—by living one day at a time.

This patient had been studying physiology in college, so she was able to relate the formation of habit patterns to her own way of life.

Today, three years later, she is married and has a child, born by natural childbirth, whom she is raising with habit patterns that emphasize eating simply and healthfully.

MAJOR TOXINS IN FOOD

10

How can habit patterns of overindulgence cause sexual malfunction?

To answer this question properly we must take into consideration each major toxic substance, or poison.

Salt

The first to consider is salt.

But we must initially understand something of the chemistry of digestion.

The food we eat helps give us blood and our blood feeds our body's cells, and thus at the very outset our concern must be with the food taken into our body.

However, when we try to classify our foods it is difficult to know where to begin. We have organic and colloidal foods; inorganic or crystalloidal foods; raw foods which may come under the heading of hydrophile colloids; cooked foods or hydrophobe colloids; and inert foods, which do no more than serve as ballast. Then there are substances which in small doses stimulate or poison insidiously, and in larger doses poison and cause deterioration of vital organs. Physiologists believe that most foods should be of a colloidal or organic nature and that the chemistry of digestion is a problem of colloid chemistry. Our attention therefore is drawn to a crystalloidal substance that is now being consumed in great quantities. I refer to sodium chloride, inorganic . . . table salt.

Long ago it was observed that, in certain states of organic deterioration, salt seemed to aggravate the condition. Now we know that it interferes with the elimination of metabolic waste products, and that it causes irritation in the prostate of the male and in the womb of the female. Dr. Alexander Haig showed that it interfered with the elimination of uric acids, causing the nephritic patient to grow more edematous. Later it was shown that in animals such as dogs, and in birds such as chickens, where a good deal of the nitrogen is eliminated as uric acid, the feeding of salt, even in very small quantities, resulted in death. Autopsy showed the liver and kidneys studded with uric acid concentrations.

Salt is a stimulant. It makes us feel good temporarily by elevating the blood pressure a little and also stimulating the adrenal glands. We say that salt is necessary for life. But is it? Let's take a closer look.

When a person is younger, it is possible for him to eliminate salt quite rapidly through such channels as the skin and kidneys. As long as the body is strong, liver and kidney function normal, resistance good, and the glands of internal secretion adequate, not much salt is retained. But when the channels of elimination are inadequate, salt retention, with its attendant harmful consequences, may result at first in functional derangement followed by organic destruction of the liver, kidneys, skin, prostate or womb, or brain, or all five.

Much brain irritation can result from diffusible poisons in the cerebrospinal fluid. Normal cerebrospinal fluid is absolutely neutral, free of diffusible substances. Nature has literally floated the brain in a bed of this fluid which serves as a cushion to protect it from damage. The spinal cord is also surrounded by fluid, which follows each nerve in its separate sheath to its final destination. Under certain circumstances, when the circulating blood is saturated with diffusible irritants, it is possible for these irritants to enter the cerebrospinal fluid.

How does normal cerebrospinal fluid get into the spaces around the brain and nerves? It is secreted by a special tissue called the choroid plexus, situated as a lining of the brain, which filters the pure water from the circulating blood through special cells. The choroid plexus is a serous membrane and, as such, is under the influence of the thyroid gland. Under extreme duress, it is possible for the thyroid to guide diffusible poisons into the cerebrospinal fluid in order to decrease their harmful concentration in the blood. Localized areas of brain tissue can be irritated by these diffusive poisons and will govern the character of the mental symptoms. For example, if a "fear center" in the convolutions of the brain is irritated, a type of insanity may develop which will cause the victim to flee from everything. He may constantly run or fight in self-defense. As the ramifications of the convolutions of the brain are most complex, almost any type of insanity can result, depending upon the exact location of the point of irritation, and the amount of irritation.

There are three kinds of diffusible irritants that can enter the cerebrospinal fluid and inflame the brain cells. First are highly diffusible electrolytes, of which sodium chloride is the most common, although other salts, such as the new sodium chloride substitutes, monosodium or potassium glutamate, and others, can be just as harmful. Quinine or its chemical derivatives or synthetic equivalents are examples of such salts.

I will cite here several patients' case histories that serve to illustrate the symptoms, and describe the treatment of salt irritation of the brain. A housewife of 32 began to suffer from spells of physical weakness and mental depression. She was well developed and healthy looking and had no particular worries. For no apparent reason she would shut herself up in her room and cry for hours at a time. When these spells became alarmingly frequent, she was taken to a psychiatrist who prescribed shock treatment. The treatments were attended by profuse sweating. Attacks became less frequent and her weakness disappeared.

But in a few months she had a relapse, so a new series of shock treatments was started. After the third treatment, with no improvement, she came to my office. A different kind of therapy was tried, a therapy based upon detoxication. Her history showed that she had always been a heavy salt-eater. Her tears, sweat, and urine contained excessive sodium chloride, a fact confirmed both by taste and by laboratory examination. I placed her on a very restricted intake of salt, and her diet, which had previously been acid, was directed toward the alkaline side. After two weeks there was a decided improvement, with no recurrence of attacks since that time. Three years have passed without the slightest mental symptoms. She works hard without fatigue. Her married life is exceedingly happy. She eschews salt.

There was also an Ohio housewife who experienced salt irritation of the womb, which nearly drove her "crazy," and salt poisoning of the brain which caused her to appear insane to her husband and family. She had two nervous breakdowns in a year and feared her husband would divorce her because she was unable to meet his sexual needs. She experienced deep moods of depression, was hospitalized and given heavy dosages of tranquilizers, which intensified her condition. After she was released from the hospital she became my patient and I suggested an alkaline diet rich in zucchini, celery, string beans, fruits, and small amounts of protein, with calcium pills to help regulate her overactive thyroid. After less than a year of faithful adherance to her diet, she was well mentally and physically, and again able to satisfy her husband sexually.

How do you know if you may be overindulging in salt? If your skin is dry and parched-looking. If you are prematurely wrinkled. If your hair is thinning or falling out. If you are bloated by water retention. These are but a few of the signs. Much can be learned from your past food history and from your habits in eating salt. Do you feel you must pour salt on everything you eat? Stop *now,* change your habit pattern consciously and replace it with a new healthful one.

Coffee

Another major source of toxicity is the habit of drinking coffee in large amounts.

Coffee comes from a little tree about twelve to twenty feet high, with red berries about the size of a small cherry. Inside the berries are two small beans pressed together so that one side of each is flat. These are coffee berries, which, when roasted, give us the fragrant brew that has become an American institution.

The original coffee tree probably grew in Ethiopia. Its culture spread to Arabia somewhere around the seventeeth century, and from there to India, Ceylon, and Java. It was not until the eighteenth century that coffee was introduced into Brazil, which today produces more coffee than the total produced by the rest of the world.

The word *coffee* comes from the Arabic word *qahwah,* through the Turkish *kahveh;* the original meaning in Arabic was "wine." It is believed that the word was first used when coffee became a substitute for the wine which is forbidden to Moslems by the Koran.

The first London coffeehouse was opened in 1652 and coffee was introduced to America in 1668.

Today the coffee that we drink is roasted. There are, in the coffee-roasting trade, about eight different "roasts": light, cinnamon, medium, high, city, full city, French, and Italian.

On the west coast of the United States coffee is made fairly "light." In the eastern part of the country it is medium, while residents of the South prefer the darkest roasts. When we speak of a coffee "blend," it is meant the mixtures of coffees from different countries, each of which has its own characteristic taste. The roasting of coffee produces very significant chemical changes in the coffee bean. Roasting eliminates the water and develops the oils that give coffee its special odor and taste.

A single cup of coffee contains some 100 to 200 milligrams of caffeine, one of the drugs known as alkaloids. An alkaloid is a compound containing nitrogen, occuring in plants and having the power of combining with acids to form salts. The caffeine in coffee begins to affect most coffee drinkers about the time they drink their sixth or seventh cup.

At present, Americans use about seventeen pounds of coffee annually per person. It is estimated that 95 percent of the families in this country drink coffee daily. Furthermore, eight out of ten adults and one out of four children have coffee daily. We are presently imbibing each year a billion more gallons of coffee than milk, three times more than soft drinks, and fifty times more than hard liquor. Again according to statistics, 25 percent of American coffee drinkers consume five or more cups per day.

We know that caffeine is a powerful poison to certain forms of life. For instance, a drop of caffeine injected into the skin of a small dog will produce death within a few minutes. An infinitesimal amount injected into its brain will cause convulsions.

The Department of Agriculture booklet *The Toxicity of Caffeine* reports research done on rabbits. Only one rabbit in ten survived injected doses of caffeine. Those that survived generally died after a second or third dose. Cats and dogs showed symptoms of poisoning which resembled poisoning from strychnine.

Almost every one of my patients has reported withdrawal symptoms when coffee-drinking was abruptly stopped. Which is, of course, typical of any addiction. As for heart trouble and coffee-drinking, many nutritionists agree that large amounts of coffee have a definite effect on the heart and blood pressure and on liver and kidney function.

Excessive use is harmful, for stimulation and irritation are closely related.

My research and experience has shown liver and kidney damage from overindulgence in coffee, as well as a general loss of energy. Sexual health depends upon a high energy level. Excessive coffee depletes energy and disturbs blood-sugar levels.

The person endangered by coffee, I believe, is the one who feels he simply can't get along without it. If he stops and soberly counts up how many cups of the beverage he imbibes in one day, he may find that coffee is indeed a drug to him. If he discovers that a few hours after drinking coffee his energy level lags and he needs more coffee, then he should cut down or, preferably, gradually cease drinking coffee until he reaches the point where he can stop altogether.

Sugar

Research scientists now recognize the importance of proper blood sugar levels to good health.

The ideal blood sugar level is one which rises a little after each meal when the body is busy digesting the food just eaten, then levels off gradually to a plateau, lowering further just before the next meal.

Most all of us know that the one sure symptom of diabetes is a high blood sugar level—medically referred to as hyperglycemia—which results when the mechanism in the body controlling the use of sugar goes awry. Veins and arteries are then over-burdened with sugar, which eventually shows up in large quantities in the urine.

Hypoglycemia, the condition of low blood sugar, is the opposite of diabetes. Low blood sugar comes about in this manner: When sugar is eaten it goes almost immediately into the blood stream because it does not need to be digested. This in some individuals raises the blood sugar level to an abnormal height. However, instead of staying at this height or leveling off to normal, the blood sugar level plunges almost immediately to a very low level. Perhaps later, the individual afflicted with hypoglycemia eats something else that contains considerable white sugar, or white flour products (such as doughnuts). His blood sugar level soars again, only to drop then far below normal or near-normal a half-hour or an hour later. Here, then, is a condition that produces a vicious cycle in which the blood sugar level, unlike diabetes, rises precipitately then swiftly and sharply drops.

In the first stages of hypoglycemia there are recurring feelings of lightheadedness, usually at mid-morning, and late afternoon. This lightheaded feeling, after a few years, can cause the hypoglycemic to react with intense anxiety, even panic and depression. In extreme cases, the hypoglycemic can reach a point of such anxious despair that suicide is contemplated. In fact, many of the victims of this shrouded disorder have been subjected to the most severe psychiatric treatments, from electric shock therapy to prolonged confinement in mental institutions.

Hypoglycemia very frequently defies detection, masquerading as epilepsy, hypochondria, or senility. Victims of this condition often seem neurotic—may, as a matter of fact, have become neurotic—though appearing healthy in every other way. Many physicians who specialize in metabolic disorders believe it affects no fewer than ten million people in the United States alone.

Recently, in the *Oxford Looseleaf Medicine,* a warning to physicians appeared. It essentially recommended that hypoglycemia should always be considered a possibility by doctors, especially those involved in neuropsychiatry. It also stated that frequently patients undergoing psychiatric treatment actually were low-blood sugar victims whose complaints of insomnia, tremors, depression, frigidity, and impotence were really being caused by their low-sugar condition.

Ironically, this condition does not stem from a lack of sugar in the daily diet but rather from the inability of the body to regulate the sugar. In a healthy, non-hypoglycemic body the blood contains approximately two teaspoonfuls of sugar, which is essential for proper functioning of the nervous system and brain.

This inability of the body to regulate the sugar level is due to overactivity of the pancreas. The United States Department of Agriculture reports that the average consumption of white sugar per person in this country exceeds one hundred pounds a year. For some people this year-after-year indulgence overstimulates the pancreas until it becomes "sensitized."

When the pancreas goes berserk and increases the insulin secretion, the sugar level drops drastically, leaving the brain and nervous system in a state of sugar starvation. Since the brain's primary source of nourishment is glucose, or natural sugar, this deprivation can alter the normal personality of its victim, turning an energetic and happy person into a depressed, worn out individual.

Sugar sensitivity is only one trigger for causing overactivity of the pancreas; the emotions too, are capable of activating the insulin release button. When a person has been subjected to a prolonged period of sustained stress, the body reacts by supplying adrenalin. Adrenalin causes the body to draw on its sugar reserve, thereby raising the sugar level of the blood. Again the pancreas over-reacts, and the too-abundant insulin brings the blood sugar level down too low.

It should be remembered that long term consumption of white sugar, white flour starches, and caffeine, whether in coffee or soft drinks, is anathema to the pancreas.

The individual experiencing low blood sugar finds little enjoyment in any area of his life. Usually, he does not have the energy to participate in or enjoy a normal sex life. For such patients I recommend five small meals a day to keep the blood sugar level regulated.

I am convinced that white sugar products and white flour starches should be cut down or eliminated entirely from every person's daily diet. Any amount of these toxin producing products are poisonous.

Alcohol

The Bible mentions the taking of a little wine "for thy stomach's sake," but many hundreds of years before that passage was written down the Egyptians used an alcoholic drink made from fermented grain. It is difficult to tell when primitive man first used alcohol. Perhaps it was after observing its effect on swine that had eaten fermented grain or fruit; perhaps he learned first-hand after having eaten overripe wild grapes.

Because of a certain amount of stimulation that occurred after its consumption, alcohol was probably the first drug used, and valued by the primitive medicine men as a relief for the weak and the sick. The Greeks made a god of Bacchus, the wine bibber and maker. Alcohol seemed to relieve pain, it produced a warm glow that seemed to dispell chills. It seemed to produce a state of mental relaxation, often inducing sleep. In small amounts it seemed to be beneficial. It could change someone who was depressed into an ecstatic, carefree, jovial person . . . and also into a terrible and dangerous human being.

Today there is deep national concern with a condition we call "alcoholism." Even in those earlier times it was noted that depression followed stimulation. The distressing symptoms of the hangover caused much fear, probably creating the first prohibitionists and the consequent war between users and nonusers that has continued through the ages. Even in the days of strictest prohibition, legal or spiritual, cunning medicine men slipped the "demon alcohol" surreptitiously into many of the popular theraputics of the day. The writings of Dr. Abraham Jacobi, who lived from 1830 to 1919, contain a list of "medicines" popular in his time. The following list shows the percentage of alcohol in some of these tonics.

Parker's Tonic	41.4% alcohol
Schrenk's	
Seaweed Tonic	19.5% alcohol
Capp's	
White Mountain Bitters .	6.0% alcohol
Green's Nervena	17.2% alcohol
Hoofland's	
German Bitters	25.5% alcohol
Kaufman's	
Sulfur Bitters	20.5% alcohol
Whickal	28.2% alcohol
Golden's	
Liquid Beef Tonic	26.5% alcohol
Hood Sarsaparilla	18.8% alcohol
Lydia Pinkham's	
Vegetable Compound . . .	20.5% alcohol
Kilmer's	
Swamp Root	7.3% alcohol

Many of the above "cures" were labeled "entirely vegetable and free from alcohol." Some were popularly called "Methodist Whiskey." Alcohol tonics will always be with us. At the present moment radio and television commercials shout the blessings of a patent medicine that contains 12 percent alcohol. It is interesting to note that the alcohol content of table wines, like burgundy (dessert wine), is usually 12 percent.

Although the concentration of alcohol in patent medicines has been lowered by law, certain vitamins dispensed in liquid form continue to contain considerable alcoholic content.

The science of endocrinology teaches that alcohol stimulates the adrenal glands and inhibits the thyroid gland. Many of the apparently pleasant symptoms that follow the drinking of alcohol can be classified as characteristic of a state of hyperadrenalism (adrenal stimulation). Both socially and physiologically alcohol is a habit-forming drug. Most people seem to be able to drink this drug without becoming alcoholics. Why do some become alcoholics? The answer seems to be in the physical-chemical makeup of the individual, though the actual reason to date remains unknown.

As alcohol is commercially made from the fermentation of sugars and starches, so also can it be made in the digestive tract. Certain chronic forms of indigestion facilitate the fermentation of sugar and starches in the intestines, resulting in a state that resembles alcoholic intoxication. Deaths follow an acute intestinal fermentation which has overstimulated the adrenals, causing a heart attack. Chronic intestinal fermentation, with excessive gas production, is a common affliction. The liver may be greatly damaged, and a state of plethora causing dilated or varicose veins may occur. The victim of intestinal fermentation may have the red face or nose characteristic of a drunkard and still be a teetotaller.

I once had a patient who was the minister of one of the largest churches in his particular town. He complained of severe indigestion and gas. His Sunday breakfast—which he ate late, just preceding his church service and sermon—was a toxic combination of the most fermenting foods. From the resulting alcoholic fermentation came stimulation and zeal; his fiery and moving sermons were the product of alcohol, literally distilled from wrong food combinations. Yet he was a staunch prohibitionist! This man, who failed to follow dietary instructions, suffered a premature death due to chronic liver degeneration.

Not only is ethyl alcohol an unnatural fuel for the body tissues; it also artificially stimulates the liver and adrenals. Thus two habits are formed, habits that grow and finally may become unbreakable. Alcohol, in physiological excess, also has a detrimental effect on the body cells. In high concentrations, commonly seen in alcoholism, it dissolves out certain phospholipoids (phosphorus colloids most vital to the nucleus of the cells, especially nerve and brain cells) and starts a slow degeneration of the brain and liver.

Of course, the progress of this degeneration depends upon the concentration of the alcohol in the bloodstream: just a mild headache at one end of the scale and delirium tremens at the other, according to the amount of circulating alcohol. The general efficiency of the body, both physical and mental, can be quite readily impaired by alcohol, a useful, agreeable person all too often being transformed into one who is wretched.

What can be done about curing oneself of the alcoholic habit? Appeal to the conscious mind, as Alcoholics Anonymous has tried to do, yes; but also work with the body chemistry. The patient must thoroughly understand the chemical background and the state of his body cells and organs, especially the liver chemistry. Assuming the problem drinker has been able to desist, the first stage of treatment often consists of rest—and the only way to rest is to lower functional strain. Even as the muscles are rested by physical inaction, so also are the liver cells allowed to recover by being relieved of digestive strain. As a doctor, I find this is best accomplished by a short fast, permitting the patient only the most appropriate antidotes—fruit juices or vegetables, as the case demands—until all liver congestion and inflammation is removed. Then the working capacity of the liver must be restored. The nuclei of brain and body cells must be renourished with the precious phosphorus that has been leached out by alcohol. This process takes time, much time, perhaps three or four years.

Investigations have shown that alcohol exerts a depressing effect on the brain, particularly its higher functions—reflection, observation, and attention. The original excitation is followed by paralysis. It starts with the elements of the nervous system known as the inhibitory fibers. The inhibitory fibers are resistances that brake and regulate the stimuli in the nervous system. They are developed in the course of an individual's life as a result of education and training. The possession of inhibitory fibers differentiates a trained from an untrained person, a scrupulous person from someone who does not restrain his impulses and passions. Under the influence of large amounts of alcohol, these controls are relaxed and the person's judgment very likely is impaired.

Alcohol does more than paralyze the inhibitory mechanisms of the nervous system. It also desensitizes the nerve endings in the penis, which causes either one reaction or its opposite for the male during the sex act. Either his penis is so desensitized that he can maintain an erection longer than usual or, if he has had *too* much to drink, he cannot achieve an erection at all (and is frequently embarrassed by sexual malfunction). The female, when inebriated often has little or no feeling in her clitoris or vagina and finds it difficult to achieve an orgasm during intercourse.

While it is better not to drink alcohol beverages at all—since it is a drug—as long as an individual is healthy, it can do no real harm if taken in moderation, and if moderation is consistently maintained. Taken in large amounts, however, alcoholic beverages can break down the liver, destroy kidney tubules, affect the brain, and inhibit the function of the sex glands in the male.

Cigarettes

Another controversial major toxin is the nicotine found in cigarettes. Cigarette smoke also contains from 35 to 61 parts per million of arsenic, a deadly poison.

In addition to nicotine and arsenic, tobacco smoke contains several other fatal poisons: hydrocyanic acid, 5 percent of carbon monoxide, pyridine, ammonia—which irritates the mucous membranes thus causing smoker's catarrah—and 1/50 of 1 percent of the very poisonous hydrogen disulfide.

Smoking is a process of dry distillation. By dry distillation we mean the transformation of dry substances into vapor. The area of maximum heat in the cigarette is the glowing zone. Here, 25 percent of the nicotine is destroyed chemically by the heat. Behind the glowing zone, in that portion of the cigarette where the tobacco is heated to a medium temperature, gases containing nicotine arise from the leaves. About 30 percent passes out into the atmosphere, while the remaining 45 percent of the original nicotine passes with the main current of smoke to the mouth. The shorter the path from the zone of distillation to the mouth, the greater will be the amount of nicotine entering the body.

A quantity of nicotine passes into the stomach with the saliva, where it inhibits the production of gastric juice. The nicotine, which circulates in the blood, may paralyze the ganglia, or switchboards, of the sympathetic nervous system.

Nicotine produces violent peristalsis and intestinal spasms as the body strives to eliminate this poison through the bowel. The blood pressure rises, and the dermal blood vessels contract, so that people who smoke excessively often have a pallid, grey appearance.

If used in excess, smoking invariably increases nervous excitability. It also masks symptoms of fatigue, causing the smoker to continue pushing himself when he should rest.

What happens when concentrated tobacco smoke is blown into the eyes? The almost immediate reaction is to withdraw from the irritation. If the smoke continues, the eyes grow red and very painful. The conjunctiva becomes swollen and there is a watery exudation, the final result being two painful, red, wet, and inflamed eyes.

If we compare the eye to the air cell of the lung (alveolus) we observe that the eye is a delicate organ, but the air cell of the lung is exceedingly more delicate and more sensitive; it also has a much richer blood and lymph supply. The membrane lining the air cell controls the chemistry of respiration. It is thin enough for gases to permeate, while the blood supply is so rich that these gases can be diffused quickly to the cells throughout the entire body. Oxygen is absorbed and carbon dioxide is eliminated. The absorption of oxygen allows for tissue oxidation, and oxidation is life. This process of oxidation in the body tissues is controlled by the internal secretion of the adrenal glands. The lungs necessarily receive a rich supply of adrenal secretion through the bloodstream. When the content of the internal secretion of the adrenals in the bloodstream is raised there is a feeling of well-being and a surcease from nervous tension, the average smoker's reason for smoking. Since the air cells, lacking sensory nerves, can register no pain to the smoker, they just lie still and silently take their beating.

The difference between the response to irritation in the eye and the air cell is dependent upon the sensation of pain. The conjunctiva of the eye is extremely sensitive to irritants and registers irritation as pain, which pain impels the smoker to move away from the source of irritation. Since the air cells of the lung contain no sensory nerves, and we therefore experience no pain, great damage can be done to these cells. However, the lung air cells do have, under the control of the solar plexus (the abdominal nerve center), a *sympathetic* nerve supply. The protective function of this abdominal area is to deliver additional adrenalin to the injured, unfeeling air cells, thus allowing for deeper and quicker oxidation and for the consequent removal of the irritating poisons.

What actually happens to these air cells? They are literally smoked. The action of smoke on the delicate air cells of the lung is quite similar to the action of smoke on a fresh ham hung in the smokehouse to be cured. The irritants the smoke contains shrivel, dry, preserve, and harden the exterior of the ham. The surface of the ham is so thoroughly embalmed and mummified that it becomes impervious to the action of bacteria, even at fairly warm temperatures. When smoke is inhaled into the lungs, the same process takes place. The lung becomes red, wet, and inflamed, and there is cough and exudation of fluid. When the stethoscope is applied, smoker's rales are heard over the entire respiratory tree. The body's defense mechanisms then are called into activity and a battle begins between the embalming effect of the smoke and the ability of the adrenal glands to neutralize the irritation and destruction. The absence of actual pain makes the victim oblivious to the damage while the gentle bath of extra adrenal secretion creates a delusion. He remains unaware that his lung lympathics are getting black with tar-like irritants, that the actual breathing capacity of his air cells has been diminished to less than one half of normal, and that his resistance to lung disease, respiratory disease, and severe infection has been decreased to less than one half of normal.

There is multiplicity of clinical evidence to prove that tobacco smoke injures the heart and blood vessels and contributes to contracting Buerger's disease, the final rotting of the blood vessels. Whether the smoker lives ten or fifty years after acquiring the cigarette-nicotine habit depends entirely upon the potential strength of his adrenal glands.

The following is a case history of one of my female patients, who was finally able to stop smoking.

She began smoking when she was 17, and smoked for eleven years. The first time she stopped she gained six pounds in a week, so she began smoking again. Eventually, she was able to ration herself to one cigarette a day, then managed to eliminate smoking completely, though she became very irritable because of withdrawal pains. Also she would wake up in the morning with a sore throat and a chronic cough. Her marital life was deleteriously affected because of nervousness and irritability. She dearly loved her husband and wanted to have a successful marriage.

I put her on a diet of vegetables, lean meats, fruit, and small amounts of starch. Her cough stopped and her sore throat gradually and then finally disappeared, as did her irritability. It took a year of the cleansing diet to rid her system of toxins. She then told me, "I enjoy my husband and family more than ever before, and food tastes so much better!"

Someone once said that cigarettes were nails in the smoker's coffin, a statement with which I completely concur.

PART II:

FOOD-RELATED PROBLEMS IN SEX

VENEREAL DISEASE OR TOXIC SECRETIONS? 11

Venereal disease (the term is derived from the name Venus, Roman goddess of love) includes several disorders largely resulting from or acquired through sexual contact. The most common of these diseases, by far, are syphilis and gonorrhea. Each is dangerous, each has its own manner of attacking the body, and each presents special problems of cure and control. In addition, there are two other types, not as common but extremely dangerous, which I'll cover later in this chapter.

Syphilis is caused by a corkscrew-shaped germ, or spirochete, called *Treponema pallidum* (from Greek and Latin words meaning "pale twisted thread"). This germ thrives in the moist environment of the mucous membranes lining the genital tract, rectum, and mouth, but expires quickly outside the human body. That the diseases may be transmitted by sitting on contaminated toilet seats thus is a fallacy. Inside the body the syphilis spirochetes multiply rapidly and cause an insidious infection that comprises two diseases in one.

The first stage of infection, called "primary" syphilis, occurs from two weeks to three months after exposure. It usually appears in the form of a hard chancre, or open sore, on the penis or in the vagina, cervix, or rectum. Lymph nodes in the genital area may be enlarged. Diagnosis can be made by examination of fluid from the chancre under a special "dark field" microscope that reveals the organisms. About a month after the chancre appears, a blood test for antibody-like substances, produced in response to the spirochete, can futher help to detect the disease.

If untreated, syphilis proceeds to a "secondary" stage, in which the spirochetes spread through the bloodstream. The original chancre may disappear, but now a rash usually appears. At the same time, further ulcerations may occur in the mucous membranes or skin.

The secondary stage may vanish after a few days or months. Many times the disease remains latent, with no symptoms and detectable only by a blood test. However, in one out of every four cases the evidence will emerge again in a vicious fashion. The spirochetes may attack the brain, causing a form of insanity identified as general paresis; they may attack the spinal cord, resulting in a type of paralysis known as locomotor ataxia; or they may strike at the blood vessels—particularly the body's main artery, the aorta—or the optic nerve, causing blindness.

Although less lethal than syphilis, gonorrhea is far more prevalent and more difficult to control. The disease is spread by a gonococcus, which thrives in the moisture of the mucous membranes. The first signs of infection usually appear within a few days after contact with the carrier. In males, the disease announces itself in the form of pain while urinating and a discharge of pus from the penis. Unless treated, the gonococci may spread through the reproductive system, inflaming the prostate gland, seminal vesicles, and testicles, possibly causing sterility.

Sometimes gonorrhea in the female remains dormant, producing no apparent symptoms. When symptoms do appear, the woman experiences burning urination and a slight vaginal discharge which may be accompanied by an overall hot, flushed feeling.

Another problem that makes gonorrhea hard to control is the number of genital infections loosely classified as non-specific urethritis, the symptoms of which closely resemble those of gonorrhea in the early stages but which are not necessarily spread by sexual contact. As infectious diseases, syphilis and gonorrhea are outranked in incidence by the common cold. However, while venereal disease (V.D.) is not therefore No. 1 among the so-called reportable communicable diseases, the number of new cases each year exceeds those of strep throat, scarlet fever, measles, mumps, hepatitis, and tuberculosis combined. Projections for 1972 indicate 624,000 new cases of gonorrhea. Considering that for every case reported four cases will remain unreported, the real figure may be over two million.

Disturbing Statistics

For syphilis, which when untreated may lead to insanity and death, the figures are even more disturbing. Today there are half a million Americans with untreated syphilis, and this year's increase includes 85,000 new cases. The number of new syphilis cases currently reported represents an increase of 16 percent over last year, the biggest increase in two decades.

V.D. seems to strike hardest in the cities, where there are at least 12 cases of syphilis for every 100,000 persons. Nationwide, Newark, New Jersey, ranks first among cities with 124 per 100,000 persons, followed by Atlanta, Georgia, and San Francisco, California. For gonorrhea, the national case rate is 308 per 100,000 population. In the Atlanta area the incidence of gonorrhea is an astronomical 2,510 per 100,000; in San Francisco 2,067. Six percent of women having babies at a major Los Angeles hospital had gonorrhea.

V.D. is particularly rampant among young Americans. At least one in five persons with gonorrhea is under 20 years of age. Last year, more than 5,000 cases were found among youngsters between 10 and 14, and 2,000 among children under 9 years of age. "The probability that a person will acquire V.D. by the time he's 25 is about 50 percent," says

Dr. Walter Smartt, former Chief of the Los Angeles County Venereal Disease Control Division.

Some of my patients have come to me with previous diagnoses that have indicated the early symptoms of syphilis or gonorrhea. Many of these had been given heavy injections of penicillin and still were not cured.

Why? Because they did not have syphilis or gonorrhea or any other venereal disease in the first place, but were plagued by toxic secretions which so often masquerade as a venereal disease. These secretions, in the prostate of the male and the womb in the female, and eliminated through the male's penis and the female's vagina, are the result not of V.D. but of general body toxemia due to overindulgence in improper food habits.

Franz Schubert wrote a song about a young couple who, while walking along the beach, stopped in an empty fisherman's hut. Their talk was serious. The man had decided to part with the woman. She was crying, and as her tears dropped upon his hands he eagerly licked them—only to be poisoned by the tears.

A case from my files, which well illustrates toxic sexual secretions and orgasms, is somewhat similar. My male patient, 46 years of age, gave the following history. His past life had been healthy, physically and sexually. In June 1970, he became acquainted with a buxom red-headed girl, a case of love at first sight. Their sex life was especially active on weekends; they were so in love that a marriage was planned. After the fifth week a despondency developed in the man while a vaginal irritation, with much increased secretion, bothered the woman. She consulted a gynecologist who discovered an inflamed vagina, which manifested itself in a yellowish-discharge, with a leukorrhea that had a putrefactive odor.

Coinciding with her problems, there arose an insatiable, abnormal desire for sex in the man, which deeply concerned him. He would have frequent erections. While seated on the toilet, he would experience semen ejaculations. His increased depression led to crying spells. Eventually, his right testicle started swelling and, although it was painless, doubled in size. By that time the girl had become extremely antagonistic toward him, and did not care to have sex or see him anymore. The engagement was broken.

He came to my office. Through a prescribed diet, after several months the man regained his health; his body returned to normal.

What had happened? The girl was extremely toxic, although only 19 years old. She had started her menses at 13. Her periods thereafter had been extremely painful, sometimes with excessive bleeding for seven days, necessitating bed rest. An excess of sugar (the consequence of ice cream, candy, soft drinks, cakes, pies, and sweet pastries) in her diet contributed greatly to this condition. The toxins were of course being eliminated vicariously through her womb and vagina. In addition to the sugar toxins, she was also eliminating putrefactive acids from an excess of cooked eggs, cheese, and rich salad dressings, which caused more mucous membrane irritation and a disagreeable odor.

She was in truth the villain and he the victim. During intercourse the man absorbed, through his penis, these toxic secretions, with subsequent inflammation of his testicle. The toxic conditions of both were aggravated by their overindulgence in sex, resulting in depletion of their adrenal glands. They soon began to repel each other, just as two similarly charged particles in a physics experiment repel each other.

Another case from my files involves a scientist I examined recently. Afraid that he had contracted a venereal disease, he was very nervous, embarrassed and frightened. His penis was covered with what appeared to be blisters. His entire genital area itched, and it pained him to urinate. Not only could he no longer enjoy what had been a very fulfilling sexual relationship with his bride but he could not understand how he had come by this condition.

Upon examination I observed that he did not have a venereal disease but a severe case of sugar poisoning. I questioned him, asking what he had been eating during the previous weeks. I was especially interested in whatever fruits he may have eaten. He admitted that the fruit season had been an usually good one; he had indulged in two to three cantaloupes a day, sometimes ate as many as six to eight plums or peaches at a time, also large amounts of grapes, several bananas, and occasionally an apple or two; and he loved fresh blueberries with sugar and cream before retiring, a time when the digestive system is at its most sluggish.

This overindulgence caused an acid condition. To complete the cycle, in addition to the toxicity, his overactive thyroid resulted in worry over his work and finances. It has long been an acknowledged fact that worrying interferes with digestion and changes the chemistry of the food eaten. So the chemical reaction of constant anxiety (he had a tendency to brood about the future) combined with an overload of fruit acids caused him to break out in blisters on his back, then his sensitive pubic area, and finally his penis.

I immediately took him off all fruit and sugar. His intake of starch was cut down to a bowl of oatmeal with unsalted butter and raw milk—his breakfast. For lunch as well as dinner, he was to have as much cleansing zucchini squash and string beans as he could eat, as well as raw celery and cucumbers, and a small amount of protein, such as rare lamb or beef, fish, or chicken.

Within a week the blisters had dried. His bride, thinking the crisis passed, forgetfully put brown sugar in his oatmeal one morning. Before the day was out, a new series of blisters appeared on his penis.

With this second crisis, I placed him on a purifying diet of zucchini squash, string beans, and celery for lunch and dinner, and also allowed some pecans. (Pecans are one of the best sources of vegetable proteins available.)

A few days later his penis and pubic area were once more free of blisters. He was delighted and so was his wife, who strictly helped maintain a proper diet. He is no longer plagued by toxic sexual secretions, and they are a very happy couple.

My most recent case of toxic sexual secretions involved a patient from Hawaii. He was very interested in yoga and had decided to go on a fruit-juice fast, taking pineapple juice only. (I always dilute fruit juice with at least equal parts of distilled water. I frequently use more than one variety of juice and voluntarily put myself, on occasion, on three-day fruit-juice fasts.) After the sixth day, he noticed that it pained him to urinate. His penis was red and swollen. He candidly told his girl friend, who agreed he should seek professional help at once. The doctor he consulted was puzzled, sure that the patient had venereal disease. The tests had come back negative. The patient was nevertheless given penicillin shots as a precaution. The condition hadn't cleared by the time he came to me. My treatment consisted of an alkaline diet. I took away all sugar and fruit, especially pineapple. Within a month, on the alkaline diet, his penis— and sex life—were restored to normal.

A major problem in the treatment of gonorrhea is that the gonococci—like the staphylococcus that plagues U.S. hospitals—have become increasingly resistant to penicillin. The standard amount of penicillin needed to effect a cure has increased during the last twenty-five years from 150,000 units to 2.4 million units per person. Large amounts can do damage to the vital organs and, even after large dosages of the drug, many cases remain uncured. An estimated 800,000 female carriers are at large today, unknowingly transmitting the disease to their sexual partners. In active cases, the disease may spread through the reproductive tract, causing painful pelvic inflammatory disease. It also scars the Fallopian tubes, a condition that represents a major cause of infertility in American women.

The male who has contracted gonorrhea may notice a burning sensation coupled with a white discharge during urination, anywhere from two days to two weeks after exposure. Often he will go to the bathroom and discover that he is unable to urinate; then he will find that he has a painfully distended bladder, and becomes panic-stricken. What has happened is that the gonorrheal infection has slowly deposited scar tissue in the urethra, and the bladder may be in danger of rupturing. When this occurs, treatment is painful. The doctor uses a stainless steel rod, about the diameter of the little finger, which he forces up the urethra as gently as possible. This opens up the tubing in the urethra and allows the urine to drain. Then the doctor replaces the rod with a rubber hose of the same diameter, which acts as a drain until the infection is healed.

One of the two other venereal diseases which I stated would be covered in this chapter is just as destructive as syphilis and gonorrhea. Called granuloma inguinale, it is caused by bacteria. Little bumps slowly break out on the surface of the genitals. Gradually, they turn into raw oozing masses of tissue spreading over the penis, labia, clitoris, anus. Once in a while, the penis, scrotum, or clitoris becomes permanently enlarged.

Because it is so insidious, granuloma inguinale is especially dangerous. The manifestations are painless, encouraging its victims to procrastinate about treatment until the condition is far advanced. Also, as much as three months may elapse between exposure and the first sign of infection, by which time the original carrier would have infected others.

Lymphogranuloma venereum (L.G.U.) is another venereal disease that, while obscure, is very dangerous. Approximately three weeks after exposure, a lump appears on the sexual organs. Two weeks later another lump, the size of an egg, appears in the groin. L.G.U. is different from all other venereal diseases in that it is the only one caused by a virus. The others develop from bacteria and, in most cases, bacteria will respond to antibiotics whereas viruses usually do not.

This venereal disease has a pronounced effect on the entire body; the victim usually feels sick. Fever, joint pains, and chills are common. The most painful reactions occur when the infection spreads from the groin's lymph glands to those around the anus. Defecation, at first painful, sometimes becomes impossible. The treatment is dilation of the anus.

L.G.U. also can cause swollen lymph nodes to break through the skin at dozens of different points. The ensuing pus continually drains through the openings, particularly in the perineum, the area between the genitals and the anus.

L.G.U. is the most difficult of the venereal diseases to treat. In fact, most medical textbooks state: "Unfortunately, no specific treatment for Lymphogranuloma venereum exists at the present time."

In summary, we find that a venereal disease not only makes for a polluted body, but that the toxemia provides an environment in which infectious bacteria may breed and multiply, and from which environment viruses are spread within the individual as well as passed on to others.

Toxic sexual secretions usually are not infectious and do not spread from person to person, as is true of venereal diseases. Toxic sexual secretions can be relatively quickly eliminated by following an alkaline diet. In most cases, venereal disease is treated by penicillin or sulfa-based drugs. V.D. also can be helped to be eliminated by cleansing the body of toxicity through proper diet and patterns of eating.

IMPOTENCE AND EGG YOLKS

12

The most accepted definition of impotence is the inability of the male to engage in sexual intercourse because of failure to maintain an erection.

There are two basic causes for impotence. The first and most widely recognized cause is that which is due to mental conditioning as a child, a poor family background, and sometimes overattachment to the mother. The second has a physical basis, toxemia in the bloodstream that affects the male sex organs.

To the boy or girl infant, the mother is the first love object outside itself. She is not only the source of pleasure but also of sustenance, safety, and comfort. This memory and feeling persists subconsciously throughout life. Many a time I have seen older or middle-aged patients who have suffered a stroke or heart attack and, in a semiconscious state, cry out for mother in a childlike voice.

The first romantic love interest of the child, which is directed toward the parent of the opposite sex, is subconsciously entwined with lust, the instinctual desire for pleasure through sensuous activities. This first sexual attraction of the boy for his mother is called the Oedipus complex, made famous by Freud, who took the term from the ancient Greek tragedy, *Oedipus Rex,* by Sophocles. The timeless appeal of this play is attributed to the fact that it enacts the fulfillment of the childish lust-wish for the parent and the subconscious guilt feelings that often follow.

The play concerns the life and fate of Oedipus, the son of royal parents. As an infant, he was abandoned to die because of a prophecy that the king, his father, would be killed by the hand of the son. Oedipus, however, was rescued and brought up by foster parents whom he believed to be his own. Later, as a young man, he received a prophecy from an oracle that he was destined to kill his father and marry his mother. Petrified, he decided to escape his fate by leaving what he believed to be his home. On the journey Oedipus encountered a stranger, an older man, who provoked a fight. Oedipus killed him.

When Oedipus arrived at the next city, he found the citizenry mourning their king, whom they believe to have been killed by bandits. The man able to solve the riddle of the Sphinx was to be their next king. The riddle of the Sphinx, an ancient secret, had never before been solved. And so when Oedipus easily solved the riddle, he was held in high esteem.

He became king, and married the widowed queen. They had several children during the years of his prosperous reign. Then a plague descended upon the city and the oracle declared that it would not be lifted until the slayer of the former king was revealed. In his search for the truth, Oedipus discovered to his horror that the stranger he killed was his own father, the king, and that the mother of his children was also his mother. Oedipus gouged out his own eyes and staggered off to self-banishment; the queen killed herself.

Because virtually every man is subconsciously touched by this story, the legend of Oedipus has lived on while other dramas just as well written have been forgotten. *Oedipus Rex* is one of the first written dramas involved with primordial sexual instincts and their subsequent expression and re-pression in the evolving social order.

Psychologically, it is believed that male impotence has its origins in an unresolved Oedipus complex. The cause of psychological impotence, often deeply rooted in the sub-conscious, involves the loss of ability to adjust to one of the basic human instincts, the sex drive. It is basically a denial of the normal function of the genitals—psychological self-castration.

Impotence, on the mental level, often exists temporarily in the male during periods of emotional stress, physical illness, loss of a loved one, financial difficulty, etc. Time and rest usually cure this situation, especially if the male has an understanding partner who is patient and loves him.

The male has difficulty getting or maintaining an erection when he is toxic and lacks sexual energy. This lack is often due to eating dead food combinations and otherwise heavily indulging in toxin-producing materials. In 50 percent of the cases that I have treated for impotence, the cause has been pure physical depletion due to toxemia-induced causes. In 35 percent of impotence cases I have treated, the cause has been both mental and physical. In only 15 percent of impotence cases was the problem solely mental, and all of these cases were the result of poor environment or problems in parental relationships, usually with the mother. Sex reeducation proved helpful in solving such cases. When there is a sincere desire and cooperation on the part of the patient, once the cause is uncovered, mental impotence usually is resolved.

Physical impotence often takes a longer period of time to treat and resolve. Early in my practice I had a patient who was courting a girl and had hopes of marrying her. He and his intended decided to spend a few days in the desert. They were up late the first night and, when they finally got in bed, he couldn't manage an erection. This condition persisted during their two-week stay in the desert. His inability to obtain an erection worried him to the point of compounding the problem emotionally.

His diet during this time included mostly dead foods—quick, easy things to prepare and eat. What he chiefly needed, diet-wise, was protein to rebuild his sex glands.

I put him on a diet of six egg yolks a day, two at breakfast and lunch, and two in the mid-afternoon. The remainder of his food program included rare meat, boiled potatoes, whole-grain bread and butter, fruit, and raw milk.

Within four months he was completely well; the egg yolks had built up his adrenals and had supplied needed phosphorus. He has now been married for fifty years to the same woman and has never again been troubled by impotence.

Another very recent case was that of a public relations man, impotent from both mental and physical causes. His early history revealed an over-attachment to his young and beautiful mother, who was a teacher and very proud of her intelligent son. The boy and his father competed constantly for the mother's attention, which she encouraged. This young man was also fed a poor diet from the beginning of childhood, very heavy in starches, causing a starch break in the liver's mechanism. He subsequently became obese. His teenage years were filled with conflict and physical illness. He had a continual break-out on his skin, an acne condition that no dermatologist—or treatment—had cured.

This patient was in his late twenties when I met him. He had dated many attractive women but was impotent with all of them. He had spent five years with a psychoanalyst, had understood and resolved his problem of mental impotence, and for a while was able to consummate his sexual relationships. Then he found himself impotent again, which confused and deeply disturbed him. I explained the function and use of the various avenues of vicarious elimination and pointed out that his prostate, acting as such an avenue, was affected by toxemia. He agreed to follow a food regime which I recommended. Within a year's time, this patient was completely cured and his sex life was very active.

Another form of temporary impotence is called "copulatory impotence." This is quite an unpleasant condition because, from all appearances, the sex act seems to be going along smoothly. Erection proceeds normally, insertion is made. Suddenly the penis becomes limp. This particular problem can be the result of lack of sexual energy caused by bad eating habits.

The most unusual form of impotence bears the name "psychogenic aspermia." The male gets and maintains a hard erection, but after insertion finds it impossible to ejaculate. The erection stays rigid sometimes for an hour or more, which usually tires the female partner.

"Premature ejaculation" occurs when the male makes contact with the vagina and has an instant climax, often before he has entered into the female. Masters and Johnson consider a man to be a premature ejaculator if he cannot control his ejaculatory process for a sufficient length of time to satisfy his partner at least 50 percent of the time. Many cases of premature ejaculation are induced by overindulgence in sweets, salt, starches, and ice cream. The prostate gland ceases to function properly because of vicarious elimination of excess sugars in its secretions.

Many years ago a patient of mine began to have problems with premature ejaculation. He loved chocolates and sweets of every kind, especially ice cream, a habit he had formed in childhood. He became addicted to chocolate.

When in his teens he attempted to have intercourse with a pretty girl, the attempt was unsuccessful; he reached an orgasm before he could introduce his penis. Each successive experience climaxed in the same way: ejac praecox (premature ejaculation).

He could not give up his habit pattern of eating large amounts of sweets. By the time he reached middle age, areas of his prostate had become atrophied or "burned out." In these areas fibroid tumors developed, much like the fibroid tumors of a sugar-irritated womb in the female. As the tumors grew larger, they compressed the posterior urethra. When finally he was unable to urinate, surgery was resorted to, after which he became completely impotent—the instance of a wasted sex life due to improper diet.

Another case history, physical in origin, concerned an artist who was brought to my office in a wheelchair, paralyzed due to an automobile accident. His wife had recently divorced him, since he was unable to satisfy her sexually. Emotionally and physically this man was the picture of defeat.

His food history revealed overdependence on soft drinks, alcoholic beverages, cigars, and large amounts of breaded, fried meats. Although the accident had been responsible for the abrupt lack of sexual energy there were other debilitating factors. My diagnosis was that protein poisoning resulting in an inflammation of the spinal column, which affected the motor nerve, was an additional reason for the lack of sexual energy.

I placed him on a simple diet. At first he was a model patient, following his diet faithfully. I decreased his cigars from fourteen to two daily. He was allowed two cups of weak coffee, black (adding cream and sugar makes a very strong, disagreeable toxic combination); also, two one-ounce jiggers of Scotch whiskey, which I felt had some therapeutic value in his particular case. After six months he began to show improvement, was back on his feet, walking with a cane.

He continued to improve, but was not fully recovered when he slipped back into his old ways. In his case, his seeming improvement was a dangerous development. Before his accident he had been a man who enjoyed night life, all forms of socializing, eating out, and drinking. Now that his sexual potency had returned and he could effect an erection, he began to indulge to excess. In a short time he was back in the hospital.

After his release he was ready to try again, fully aware that the diet had helped to restore his health. In a matter of months he was again walking normally, enjoying swimming; his sexual potency had returned. With the full return of his capacity to participate in the sex act, the ex-wife, who had deserted him in his extremity, now wanted to come back into his life. But there was retribution of a sort. She found to her chagrin that she had been replaced by another woman, who had helped him during his illness.

Until studies of relatively recent years and the publication of works on sexual research, it was believed that Nature caused man to become impotent as he advanced in years. But as Wilhelm Stekel, M.D., states in his study *Impotence in the Male:*

> Even in eunuchs and men who are deprived of their testicles, which frequently occurred in the War, there still exists a full capacity for erection and orgasm. The capacity for orgasm is maintained until death, as is shown by numerous observations. Also, the testicles of octogenarians frequently still show living spermatozoa. But even in the absence of spermatozoa, the capacity for erection is fully preserved.
>
> The age limits of masculine potency are remarkably high. I am coming more and more to believe that a normal man ought to maintain his potency into advanced age.

In summary, impotence, from my view of it, is primarily the result of ignorance in matters of diet, nutritional education, and a lack of sex education (which should start in childhood). Many cases of temporary impotence, such as premature ejaculation, result from fear, guilt due to sexual superstition, or selfishness on the part of the male and his lack of consideration for the orgasmic release of the female. I firmly believe that impotence, in the majority, is curable.

SEXUAL FRIGIDITY AND SWEETS

13

"Ignorance is bliss" is an old adage that is no longer true, especially when it applies to today's woman. The modern woman is aware that she has as much right to sexual fulfillment as the male.

Unfortunately, a large percentage of the female population is frigid and unable to fully enjoy sex life. *Webster's New World Dictionary* defines frigidity as "the state of habitually failing to become sexually aroused." Generally speaking, frigidity means an inability to enjoy sexual love. It is a form of sexual anesthesia which results in a lack of orgasm, the physiological response that brings sexual intercourse to its natural climax. In a true orgasm the female builds to her height of physical tension, then there is an explosive release that is manifest in a series of muscular spasms. Sometimes this orgasm is clitoral. In a full climax these spasms take place within the vagina itself, soothing the body with waves of pleasure felt throughout the entire body.

Many psychologists are convinced that sexual frigidity in the female is usually the result of some traumatic emotional experience that occurred in infancy, childhood, or adolescence. I have discovered through research and experience with my women patients that frigidity is not usually caused by mental and emotional conditioning in childhood. In 75 percent of my cases, frigidity is the result of an improper diet, which causes a poor chemical (toxemic) background due to careless eating habits during the formative years, especially during the adolescent period.

There are two stages of biological and psychological development that every person undergoes. The first lasts from birth to about 10 years of age. The second stage starts around the age of 10 and should end with the complete psychological and biological maturation of the female.

The first stage is divided into two phases. First comes the phrase known as infancy, which covers the first five years of life. Then follows the latency period, which occupies the second five years of life.

It has been scientifically established that, during the infantile period, the baby has strong sexual feelings. This sexual drive is centered in the genitals from the outset. The baby girl will masturbate by the manipulation of her clitoris. She has no awareness of her vagina as a sensual area. The sexual feelings of infancy increase in intensity after the second or third year. In a very real sense the strong sexual feelings experienced at this age set the mold for the later sexual development of the child.

During the first three years the little girl is deeply attached to her mother. In the sense that infants "know" things, the little girl knows her mother is the source of all her security. These feelings have a very clear sensual nature. The little girl loves to be close to her mother, to be stroked by her, to have her mother clean her genitals and bathe her. She associates her masturbation with these pleasant reactions. It is extremely important during these initial three years that the little girl be given a diet rich in alkaline elements. If she is overfed with proteins, starches, and foods concentrated with sugar and salt, she will in time become toxic and have local irritations of acid secretion in her vagina. The itching and soreness of such irritations may cause the child to scratch or stroke her clitoris excessively; or it may cause the child to associate pleasurable sensations with painful sensations, which later may produce difficulties of a psychological nature.

Around 3 years of age the little girl becomes aware of a growing attachment to her father. His tenderness toward her and his play with her stimulate her whole being, and her sensuality becomes increasingly attracted to him. At first she is not aware of the conflict in this attachment; but as her developing mind becomes more aware of reality, she begins to sense that her increased sensual response to her father has placed her in competition with her mother. Another woman has a prior claim on her first man! At this point she develops hostile feelings toward her mother.

Unbelievable, you might say; a little girl competing with her mother for her father's love? No, just a part of Nature's plan for normal development, preparing the child for the day when she will become a mother and start the cycle all over again.

A question that goes to the heart of the matter is this: If the early situation causes a conflict in the little girl which can lead to a neurosis later, why has Nature designed things this way? Nature is supposed to foster growth, not hinder it.

The fact is that Nature did design this early sexual conflict for a very special reason.

To reiterate: At first the little girl's feelings are focused on the mother. Mother is the center; the little one looks to her for food, security, and love. This love soon becomes tinged with erotic feelings, connected with the little girl's growing sensuality. It is necessary for humans to love and to have erotic feelings centered on others. But clearly, if this earliest love situation did not change at some point, the little girl would grow up to have woman as her erotic center of interest. Nature intends no such end result. Nature intends these erotic feelings to become man-centered. Thus, the role of the father in the child's development becomes all-important. He is the first bridge from the infantile, erotic, and dependent relationship with the mother to mature relationships with the members of the opposite sex. There are several other bridges the growing girl must cross on the road to maturity. Ultimately, she will have to give up her father, too, as the center of erotic interest, though he may probably remain in her unconscious life as the model for her future husband.

Unfortunately, *sometimes* the little girl is rejected by her mother and becomes overattached to her father. Therefore when she becomes an adult, she has relationships with older men—but remains frigid, for each man is her father, a subconscious fact deeply repressed.

Such was the history of one of my patients who was frigid due to both mental and physical causes. She was an actress who would go through periods of deliberate weight gain followed by extreme anxiety and depression. Both her emotional and physical health were in jeopardy when she arrived at my office.

She was the first child of an emotionally unstable mother, who resented being burdened with a child. The mother was a stern, cold woman whose husband, twenty years older than she, was a father figure. The father adored his little girl and centered great attention on her. This caused the mother to compete with the child and further reject her during the period when the daughter most needed her mother's love.

The father was a sensual man who loved good food, and he rewarded his young daughter with constant treats of ice cream, chocolate candies, pies, and pastries. Thus at an early age she combined (and confused) love and comfort with sweet and soft foods.

My patient's father would also have his daughter sit on his knee every evening. He would stroke her hair and kiss and fondle her, which aroused her newly awakened instincts.

She once recalled a scene for me from her early childhood. One day she and a little friend were playing in a neighborhood park. They saw an older man standing behind a clump of bushes. He beckoned to them; curious, they walked over to where he was standing—masturbating. My patient admitted that, even though she couldn't have been more than 5 or 6 years old, she felt a definite sexual pleasure at seeing the man's erect penis.

Her mental conditioning, and the poor body chemistry being formed because of overindulgence in sweets and starches, were setting the foundations for her frigidity and attraction to older men when she grew into adulthood.

The end of the first phase and the start of the second (which as we have seen lasts until about 10 years of age) begins with a remarkable psychological event: the early infantile sexuality goes completely underground. The child's masturbation stops and she forgets—actually represses—her previous feelings of erotic attachment. She enters into approximately a five-year period of nonsexuality. This new phase into which the young girl has now entered is called the "latency period," because the sexual feelings have become repressed or latent. The latency period is characterized chiefly by an attempt on her part to understand and master her environment. It is marked by tremendous growth, physically and mentally. She is interested in and fascinated by everything that gives her a chance to advance herself physically: skipping rope, doll-playing, ball-playing, swimming, climbing, running.

Nature's Intention

What she does, feels, or thinks in this period distinguishes her not too vastly from a boy of the same age.

You may ask then: What is Nature's intention in having the girl go through this latency period? The answer is that Nature gives the child a chance to grow mentally, to learn to master her body and mind, to integrate the earlier phase of development, to learn to form personal relationships, so that when she comes to the next decisive step in development, the stage marked by menstruation and female maturation, she will be ready for that development.

The latency period is also marked by close relationship to

the parents, especially the father. However, there are now no conscious sexual feelings attached to him, though she admires and values her father above all others; she wants his admiration and high regard. Most fathers give their daughters a great deal of love and reassurance during this time, and the girl basks in his love and attention like a flower drinking in the sunshine. She strives to do everything that will please him, make him notice her, make him love her. His responses are studied carefully. Thus she experiences how to "please her man," a very important factor in her development toward complete womanhood with its varied psychological give-and-take. If the father seriously fails in his role during this period, he can do much harm to the growing girl.

During the latency period the daughter has repressed her guilt feelings toward her mother, along with all of her directly sensual feelings, and during the latency period Mother emerges as a model to imitate. After all, Mother is married to the man the little girl prizes most highly in the world.

During the latency period, my actress patient lost her mother; actually, her mother left her father and went to live a life of her own. This young lady's father now became both mother and father to his daughter. The little girl thus was drawn even closer to her father. He would take her to movies, after which they would indulge in banana splits or hot fudge sundaes. The child was allowed to have dessert even if she didn't eat any dinner.

The heavy concentration of starch and sugar began to manifest themselves in her physical health. She had one cold after another, with ear infections every winter. She lacked energy. Even though born with a strong body (she is an adrenal-pituitary type), there were already signs of frigidity and the breakdown to come a result of combined psychological and nutritional stresses.

The next stage of development starts approximately at the age of 10 and should end with complete physical maturation, psychological and biological; she is now a woman.

This stage is divided into two parts or phases. The first, called puberty, lasts until 13, 14, or 15; the second we call adolescence, one of the most interesting and exciting chapters in the life history of the young woman.

At the outset of puberty, which occurs over a span of from twelve to twenty-four months, changes take place so important that they affect the entire future behavior of the individual. During this time, if normal endocrine secretion is lacking, there results an immature human being. The pity is that once these months have passed, once the "concrete has been set," there is only a slim chance to remold or repair any defects in the individual.

I speak especially of the adrenal, the thyroid, and the sex glands. There are three types of glandular deficiency that may retard proper development. The first is observed in the child whose endocrine debility is hereditary; the second in the child whose glands as a result of improper diet have been damaged by severe childhood diseases. When there are these deficencies, such a scarcity of available secretion exists that the individual cannot attain proper development during adolescence. The third class, most commonly observed, is the result of certain metabolic disturbances, primarily of the liver, which exhaust the glands of internal secretion.

When the liver fails as a mechanism of defense, toxins arising primarily in the gastrointestinal tract get into the general circulation and can damage and deplete the thyroid and adrenal glands. If these endocrines are in a depleted state, the extra secretion so important to adolescent development simply can't be supplied and proper maturation most likely will not take place.

Signs and symptoms of immature sexuality are observed more frequently in girls than in boys, probably because the male has larger adrenals. The size ratio is about three (male) to one. This proportion is also found in animals, some males having adrenals six to ten times larger than females. As a general rule, the female does not have a great surplus of glandular secretion. When depletion occurs, the results of this depletion are observed, for example, in diseases such as tuberculosis, exophthalmic goiter (with its great thyroid depletion), dementia praecox, and in severe emotional states.

Normal changes occur during the maturation of the female. First come breast changes. In addition to enlargement and nipple development, there must be strong power of nipple erection and sensory response to proper stimulation. In normally developed teenagers the tone of the breast is firm. Next are the changes in the genital organs. The clitoris enlarges, assumes power of erection, and develops intensified tactile sensation. The clitoris, analogous to the penis in the male, really a miniature penis, is situated in front of the vaginal entrance. Its tip is normally very sensitive in a healthy female. The labia, or lips of the vagina, enlarge and are supplied with delicate sensory nerves. The vagina itself enlarges; the mucous glands and the glands of Bartholin hypertrophy and acquire the ability to respond to proper stimulation. The uterus enlarges and the cervix becomes sensitive. Finally, and most important of all, orgasm is made possible. Therefore, one can easily appreciate the tremendous importance of normal endocrine balance during puberty.

Hyposecretion of endocrine glands and frigidity are linked. Some students and statisticians have placed the proportion of immaturely developed females as high as 65 percent. I think that figure should be somewhat higher, especially when we realize how rarely the physician sees a "normal" breast, and how often genital sensation is lacking, with the exception of a small amount around the clitoris. The physician, who daily listens to intimate family histories, unfortunately observes that the majority of his female patients present some sexual problem. We are becoming more than ever convinced that complete sexual maturity in the female is rare.

Weston A. Price, D.D.S., whose monumental book, *Nutrition and Physical Degeneration,* sums up many years of careful study of the effect of improper food upon the development of certain body tissues, showed that, in addition to dental defects, one of the first results of a faulty diet of too much sweets and starches is found in the complications and increasing difficulties of labor, as well as a tendency toward infertility. Students of animals state that in off-years, when deer suffer from an insufficient food supply, as many as 25 percent of the does are barren.

Dr. Francis Pottenger, Jr., while conducting his remarkable experiments on cats, which were fed solely on a cooked protein diet, noted that it was impossible for the third generation to conceive at all. Even when these third-generation felines were placed on a normal raw protein diet, it remained impossible for them to conceive. This means that the early damage to the genital glands, due to wrong diet, is sometimes irreparable.

Perhaps the most valuable and conclusive experiments were conducted by Hans Selye. He showed that estrus (the preparation of the human and animal egg cell) can be retarded, even stopped entirely, by depleting the thyroid and adrenal glands with such toxic agents as formaldehyde or through a toxic diet. I quote from an article entitled *The Effect of Adaptation to Various Damaging Agents on the Female Sex Organs of the Rat,* in which he says: "Insufficient food intake has been shown to cause irregularities of the cycle of permanent anestrus in the guinea pig and rat. In women, permanent amenorrhea [cessation of menstruation] . . . was frequently seen among the starving population of Central European countries during the First World War."

It takes a very slight stretch of the imagination to be aware that during puberty the adaptation energy or, to put it in simpler terms, the sum total of available adrenal and thyroid secretions, can be used up fighting toxins so that not enough is left for proper sex maturation during the *only time* that sex maturation is possible.

This is exactly what happened to my actress patient during her adolescent period of growth. Her body was continually fighting to eliminate toxic poisons, which left her little energy to mature properly. She was already thirty pounds overweight by the time she was 15 and a sophomore in high school. Her diet consisted of chili hot dogs and tacos for lunch, plus one or two soft drinks, and sometimes pie for dessert. On the way home from school she consumed one or two ice cream bars and a bag of potato chips. Sometimes she ate one or more chocolate bars and drank soft drinks until suppertime.

Her father would prepare spaghetti and garlic bread for dinner, or one of his other favorite meals, such as chili con carne or macaroni and cheese. As a result, he was forty pounds overweight.

His daughter had her first love affair when she was 18. She admitted freely to me that it was an unpleasant experience; she had no feeling in her breasts, clitoris, or vagina. She felt completely numb during the entire experience. She didn't even realize that it was natural and normal to actually enjoy intercourse.

Her father died when she was in her early twenties. She went through a state of shock and grief so intense that she came close to having a nervous breakdown. He had been the center of her world and she was completely dependent on him. Now, she was totally unequipped to cope with even the smallest problems.

She had two subsequent love affairs with men, one who was twenty and the other thirty years her senior. Both proved to be unsatisfactory, as she was still frigid.

She had managed to lose weight by taking pills, shots, and large amounts of thyroid extract. Her weight between acting assignments vacillated from normal to thirty and forty pounds above normal.

My actress patient hadn't worked in over a year when I first met her. Her last role had been as co-star in a film. She had collapsed on the set and had to be replaced. She had very little interest in life and had come to me as a last resort. The physical examination showed a young woman seventy pounds overweight. Her heart was somewhat off balance because of elevated vein pressure (plethora). The second pulmonic valve sound was 50 percent exaggerated, and closed with a loud snap. Her hemoglobin was only 60 percent.

I cautioned her to do no heavy physical exercise. I didn't want to frighten her, but she was in danger of having a heart attack. She was also suffering from malnutrition and anemia, and was having spells of dizziness. Her eyesight was blurring because of the heavy toxemia caused by starch, sugar, and protein poisoning. Her hands and feet were always cold from liver damage. She was in pain and continually tired.

I placed her on a program tailored to suit her individual needs. For breakfast she was to have one glass of diluted apple juice, followed by another glass midmorning. For lunch she had a salad made with cucumbers, celery, butter lettuce, and a dressing of olive oil and vinegar half and half. She also had two soft-cooked egg yolks with one pat of unsalted butter, and three or four zucchini squash. Midafternoon, she had a banana. Dinner was the same as lunch. In less than three months she had lost forty pounds.

I went on my summer vacation and when I returned found she had suffered a setback, having regained part of the weight. We corrected this problem. Since then her weight has remained normal.

Sexual Feelings Awakened

Because she had inherited an exceptionally strong body and is quite young, in less than two years' time with the help of an alkaline-rich diet her sexual feelings awakened. Recently, she happily told me of her first orgasmic climax, with a man only a few years her senior. Her dependence on a father figure has disappeared, along with her other symptoms.

Sometimes frigidity, as I mentioned earlier, is purely physical and caused by toxemia, as in a recent case which involved a music teacher, the mother of three children. She came to me in tears. She was very nervous and depressed; she was afraid of losing her husband because she felt she could no longer make a pretense of enjoying intercourse with him. She had lost all feeling. I determined that she was suffering from sexual anesthesia, caused by acute toxemia.

The deep emotional conflict and her poor dietary background were causing migraine headaches, nausea after eating, constant backaches, and sharp stabbing pains in her heart. She said she felt like a hamster in a cage, running about in a vicious circle. Her concern about her sex life caused her to eat compulsively; she had gained sixty pounds in two years. Diagnosis showed that the toxemia was being eliminated in the form of acid secretions through her womb and vagina, causing numbness in her genitals.

I explained the cause of her frigidity, then gave her a simple diet of one glass of distilled water and fruit juice, half and half, for breakfast and again at midmorning. Lunch included steamed zucchini squash, string beans, and two soft-cooked eggs. For dinner she was to have rare beef, or lamb, vegetables, and salad.

A month later she had lost thirteen pounds; however, she complained that she still had no feeling in her genitals and was unable to reach orgasm. It took two years of strict discipline, and a loss of sixty pounds, to correct this condition. Today she is a new woman, and appreciates her husband, with whom she recently returned from a second honeymoon, more than ever before.

Another one of my cases, illustrating frigidity caused by physical symptoms alone, was that of an attractive thyroid-type housewife. She was in good health until the age of 24, when she first noticed a mild ache in her elbows. She consulted a specialist who told her she was suffering from rheumatoid arthritis.

For three years she went through drug therapy, including the use of cortisone. During this time a cataract formed in her left eye; an operation was performed, which was followed by an infection that resulted in total blindness in that eye. She continued drug therapy for four more years. By this time she was in such pain that she couldn't sleep at night.

After she decided not to take drugs, she found a book on diet and tried to follow it herself. During this time she became pregnant. Following the birth of her child, all of her

joints became painful and inflamed. Her joints were deformed and some were ankylosed (as though frozen stiff).
Her knees were as large as footballs and would scarcely bend.
There was fever in her knees and ankles, with swelling of the
lower legs. Her heartbeat was rapid, her blood pressure low,
her energy level zero. She wanted her husband to put her
away in an institution, wanted him to remarry, wanted to
have her mother care for the baby.

When she came to me the acids in her blood were injuring
her kidney tubules, destroying her red blood cells, and
robbing her liver of valuable sodium. The thyroid was still
valiantly trying to sidetrack her poisons into the middle skin
(joint linings) but it was a losing battle. Here was a really
tired human being who could not be whipped or stimulated
any more. But there was still a sparkle in her one good eye
and a desperate resolve to go down fighting.

I prescribed that she fast on a simple vegetable soup for
one week and stay in bed. At the end of the week there was
practically no improvement in her joints, but she had been
able to sleep without pain for the first time in four years.
This encouraged her greatly and for the next two years,
during much trial and error, and as her diet was carefully
regulated, the pain began to leave her joints, the acids in her
blood disappeared, and many of the deformed joints began to
straighten and function normally again. In three years her
weight had returned to normal, and there was no sign of
arthritis.

She recorded in her diary the first time she went to the
market, the first time she went to the park, the first time she
could again function normally as a wife. With her health
restored, life was very full and beautiful.

In 75 percent of the cases I have treated for frigidity I
have learned by experience and research that the primary
cause has been toxemia resulting from improper diet and a
poor chemical background.

I have treated physical frigidity successfully by prescribing
individual diets that have cleansed the toxemia from the

body, restoring liver and kidney function to normal. Once the female's toxemia has been eliminated, she is capable of enjoying the benefits of the heightened feelings and the orgasms that are rightfully hers.

HOMOSEXUALITY AND LESBIANISM

14

Homosexuality in both male and female remains an area that requires much further research. I disagree with many of the current sex authorities who state that homosexuality is a mental or psychological problem only. I believe that the basis for an individual's turning to homosexuality may often be physical, the result of injury to the sex center of the brain.

The brain can be divided overall into three parts: a sex center, a digestive center, and a locomotor center. The sex center may be further subdivided into the head brain and the solar-plexus brain. The head brain controls the eyes, ears, nose, and mouth, and the ability to become sexually aroused. The strength and power to act comes from the power of the solar-plexus, the abdominal nerve center, the action dependent upon the ability of the adrenal glands to function. The brain sex center cannot function without cooperation from the pituitary and thyroid glands.

Unfortunately, in a few cases, a pregnant mother may have taken a drug like Thalidomide or some other harmful substance. Such drugs, together with large amounts of food toxins, poison nerve development centers in the unborn baby, resulting many times in irreparable nerve and brain damage.

It is a scientific fact that the largest part of the anterior brain contains the sex center. Some of my conclusions concerning this sex center have resulted from my observing persons who have sustained head injuries. I remember the case, long ago, of a man who was kicked in the head by a mule. The whole front part of the brain was kicked off but, by some miracle, the hemorrhage was stopped and the wound finally healed. There resulted no diminution in mental functions, such as the ability to think and move, but the man's sex function was altered.

I have also observed that, when certain operations are performed involving the anterior part of the brain, sex functions have been impaired, altered, or completely destroyed.

A lesion resulting from a state of toxemia can occur almost anywhere in the brain. It is my belief therefore that an undetermined percentage of homosexuality is the result of destructive lesions in the sex center located in the anterior brain.

When nerve and brain functions have been interfered with—because of toxemia or injury—there is no chance of repair, especially when the nerves are atrophied.

In many of these cases of nerve atrophy and brain damage, the conditions have occurred while the mother is still pregnant. To lessen the chance of brain and nerve injury to her child, and to contribute toward a sound mind and body, it is the mother's responsibility to not indulge in drugs and to be careful of her diet while she is pregnant.

I do agree with authorities on sex matters that many cases of homosexuality are due to early, distorted, faulty mother-son and father-daughter relationships. For instance, Dr. Alexander Lowen, in his book *Love and Orgasm,* remarks that, in the case of the male homosexual, analytic experience suggests that the combination of a seductive, close-binding mother and a rejecting father is often responsible for a homosexual son.

One of my patients grew up in this particular pattern. He lacked an acceptable male image after which to pattern his masculinity. But, more significantly, he overidentified with his mother and was unconsciously sexually involved with her. The result was an exaggeration of the Oedipal situation, to a point where the patient could not resolve his incestuous feelings for his mother.

In such situations, to reduce guilt the child often feels he must sever all sexual feelings, "deaden" his body, so to speak. Such a striving of course makes for inner conflicts, and also can be a cause toward homosexuality.

This same patient complained on his first visit to my office of arthritic pain in his entire body, and he was concerned because of his impotency. Though living with another man, having a "love affair," he could no longer get an erection. His partner was already threatening to find another lover.

At the end of his first visit and examination, I prescribed a highly alkaline diet to cleanse his body, to restore liver and kidney function, and to relieve his arthritic condition.

After a few office calls he became sufficiently relaxed to say that his lover had left. He admitted he felt relieved, not troubled, by the other man's departure. He added that at the other man's leaving he noticed within a short time his potency had returned. I suggested that perhaps his temporary impotence might be an indication that the homosexual way of life was not for him. He agreed, and as he continued to see me for checkups, we would talk. The arthritis was cured within a year and a half. As he began to understand how his relationship with his mother had caused his conflicts, he was freed from the past. Today, he has a few very fine friendships with the opposite sex, and he told me recently that some day he would like to get married.

There are basically two kinds of homosexuals. The first can identify only with members of their own sex; there is a revulsion toward the opposite sex, for reasons usually stemming from childhood.

The second kind are ambisexual. They usually enjoy

relationships with the opposite sex until situations of stress are presented, then they turn to one of their own sex for sexual release. During these periods, there is a withdrawal from and even hostility toward the opposite sex. After the pressure is removed and the environment again becomes tranquil, normal sex relations sometimes are resumed with females.

Homosexual affairs produce varying degrees of shame, self-reproach, and feelings of guilt. Many times a drive for self-destruction, such as alcoholism, has its roots in homosexuality.

Homosexuality should be understood and not condemned. Each individual in society has the right to choose his means of sexual expression as long as he does not mentally or physically hurt another human being.

MENSTRUATION AND MENOPAUSE

15

Menstruation is the regular periodic discharge of blood from the uterus (womb), recurring about every four weeks from puberty to the menopause, except during pregnancy and lactation. Menstruation has been likened to the weeping of a disappointed uterus after Nature has prepared the soil for the fertilized ovum. When the ovum remains unfertilized, the preparatory bed has to be cast off.

The age at which menstruation begins varies greatly, according to climate and region. It is generally considered that the colder the climate, the later the first menstruation. However, studies have shown that in some of the most northerly tribes of Indians and Eskimos menstruation appears as early as it does in the Tropics. The most likely explanation is that maturity depends upon the rate of internal secretion from the adrenal glands. Hot weather and a high protein diet are both adrenal stimulants. The Eskimos and the Indians of the North live almost entirely on animal food, a diet that would tend to stimulate the adrenals. This stimulation, in turn, could be the cause of bringing on menstruation at the age of 8 to 10 years, the usual beginning age among these people. On the other hand, Laplander girls do not begin to menstruate until they are 16, 17 or 18. But the Laplanders include dairy products and vegetable proteins (less stimulating than meat proteins) in their regular diet. In the Tropics the heat from the sun's rays, in spite of the preponderance of fruit and vegetables in the diet, stimulates the adrenals, so that menstruation begins as soon as it does with the Eskimos.

The duration of the menstrual flow as well as the amount of flow are greatly influenced by the diet and physical life of the individual. It is reported that among one primitive people in the Australian bush country, who live entirely upon fruit, the menstrual period lasts about twenty minutes; approximately a tablespoonful of blood is expelled. It would appear that the more complicated the diet, the more complicated is menstruation. The women of the American Indians of the Great Plains, who lived on a simple diet and were exceedingly active, had a short, uncomplicated menstrual period, scarcely noticeable. Even childbirth was easy, rapid, and free from intense pain. An American pioneer physician stated: "I have known a Sioux squaw to go after wood in midwinter, have a child while gone, wrap it up, place it on the wood, and bring both to the lodge, miles distant."

At puberty the ovaries awaken. As their internal secretion filters into the general circulation of the blood, certain changes occur. Axillary and pubic hair develop. The breasts and nipples enlarge. The womb is prepared to receive the fertilized egg cell.

About once a month a portion of the lining of the womb becomes engorged with blood, which makes it ready to receive the seed. In this blood-rich bed, the fertilized egg can absorb the nourishment it needs for its implantation and development. At this time the follicle of the ovary that has held the mature egg ruptures. The liberated ovum is propelled down the right or the left ovarian tube. During this journey down the tube, it can become fertilized by an active spermatozoon which has migrated from the vagina through the womb and into the tube. If no sperm are present, the ovum cannot be activated and attach itself to the expectant womb, so it is washed away. Then the congested area sloughs off; the blood is released and menstruation begins—a physiological process which should not take more than two days.

Because of the regularity of the menstrual cycle, many people believe that the female can be impregnated only at certain times of the month. The Mosaic law demanded that the woman should remain untouched for seven clear days after the cessation of menstruation. This was in part because she was considered "unclean" until seven days had passed.

Premature Discharge

From the moment the unfertilized egg is discharged the woman is usually immune to pregnancy. However, there are exceptions. Heightened sexual excitement, for example, can result in a premature rupture and discharge of the unfertilized egg, which would render the woman susceptible during the so-called immune period.

Other glands of internal secretion play important parts during the menstrual cycle. The ovaries make menstruation possible. The thyroid determines the interval, usually twenty-eight days. Sometimes, for example, women develop horizontal white lines—called menstrual lines—on the fingernails. These represent dead areas, indicating that growth of the nail cells was halted during the drain on the thyroid due to menstruation. Also, it is not unusual for adolescent girls to cease menstruating during an exciting trip, probably a result of the sidetracking of thyroid energy into other fields of activity, resulting in a paucity of secretion. The adrenal glands insure a rich oxygen supply to the congested womb. They also regulate the clotting of the blood, thus protecting against serious hemorrhage during menstruation.

There is a great deal of difference between what are known as average and normal conditions of health. Blinded by the idea that the average represents the normal, people have been led to believe that many pathological states are normal because they are prevalent. That is why abnormal menstrual functions are usually overlooked and endured, the average being accepted as the normal. For example, heavy cramping and lower back pain is considered normal, when actually it is abnormal. When a woman follows a clean diet she experiences little or no cramping and no back pain.

The female suffering from a state of toxemia, with her liver failing to filter as it should, places a burden on the natural menstrual function. Instead of being free to fulfill its natural purpose, this function is turned into a sort of garbage filter, resulting in a condition of chronic inflammation of the womb. If there are years of trying to help cleanse the blood of irritating toxins, the womb can become so tumerous or degenerate that hysterectomy may offer the only solution.

A study of the average female's menstrual function shows that pains or cramps and excessive flow are so common that a host of popular patent medicines are offered for their relief. When toxic blood seeks an outlet through the womb via the menstrual function, the resulting inflammation and irritation to the delicate mucous membrane throw the organ into spasms which are registered as pain or cramps. If the toxin is milder or more dilute, the patient simply feels heavy or congested in her pelvis. Once the flow has started, Nature pours out as much toxic material from the blood as possible. This inflames the deeper layers of the womb. What should be a normal flow develops into a hemorrhage, sometimes lasting for days and reducing the patient to a state of anemia. The womb, boggy after such chemical poisoning, is easy prey to harmful bacteria.

This same irritation can lead also to tumor formation. Catarrhal inflammation in the Fallopian tubes resulting from vicarious elimination can so modify those structures that the descending egg cell will be killed in the uncongenial media. This inflammation also can cause stricture of the tubes, resulting perhaps in permanent sterility. Sterility likewise can be caused by the chronic, inflamed state of the womb, which renders it unfit for the implantation of the fertilized egg. Or, even though the egg cell becomes implanted, it may later blacken and die, aborting because of the toxic chemical surroundings.

Milder states of toxemia, though not resulting in sterility, can cause chronic inflammation and hypersensitivity of the female organs. As the egg gradually develops and the time approaches for the ripe ovum to be liberated by the rupture of the Graafian follicle, the concentration of the internal secretion of the ovaries rises in the bloodstream. Toxins that have been temporarily sidetracked into the body tissues and into such organs as the lymph glands, spleen, liver, subcutaneous tissues, skin, muscles, and bones are mustered and thrown into the bloodstream. They seek vicarious elimination through the menstrual flow. The patient feels heavy and congested in the pelvic area. There is a slight rise in temperature, which means that the adrenal glands have increased oxidation in an effort to burn some of the toxic material. The pulse becomes rapid; the palms sweat; nervousness and insomnia follow.

All these symptoms derive from hyperactivity of the thyroid gland. The thyroid is making its effort toward detoxicating by liberating thyroidin into the blood, the iodine content of this secretion neutralizing the toxic material and hastening its elimination through the skin as sweat, acne, or rashes. The pituitary gland may swell as a result of oversecretion. This causes pressure against its confining bony cup (sella turcica) at the base of the brain, resulting in migraine headaches. The rising toxemia of the blood leads to liver congestion, elevation of vein pressure, and distressing fatigue. The kidneys may not be able to filter certain diffusible poisons, so that a mild to severe edema occurs, evidenced by an increase in body weight. This type of bloating at the menstrual period is very common. As the flow begins, a great deal of the toxic material is eliminated in the escaping blood. The patient is relieved, but the delicate organs have suffered a blow. Often they do not have sufficient time to recover completely before the next period begins; they therefore remain in a chronic condition of inflammation, which may lead finally to hysterectomy.

The quality of the menstrual blood varies according to the chemistry of the toxic material. Bright red, profuse, odorless blood accompanied by severe uterine cramps indicates that the preponderant irritant comes from improper digestion of sugars and starches. The offending toxins are acids which have not been completely oxidized to carbon dioxide and water, acids such as lactic, acetic, pyruvic, oxalic, and formic, to mention a few. On the other hand, if the menstrual blood is dark, odorous, clotted, and stringy, the toxins of protein indigestion or putrefaction are present. Eggs, cheese, and overcooked meat can cause most offensive odors in the menstrual blood. Thus, it is obvious that the womb, which Nature selected as the organ of reproduction, can, under chemical duress, become an organ for the elimination of putrid waste. Women proverbially live longer than men. Perhaps one of the reasons is that they are, to one degree or another, cleansed from toxemia by the regular menstrual function.

The toxemia-afflicted woman not only endures much suffering during her menstrual years, she faces an even more difficult ordeal at the menopause. The normal menopause in the healthy woman is almost symptomless. But the toxic female who has had relief from the burden of her poisons through menstrual channels truly suffers as a whole series of new ailments arise: menopausal hot flashes, extreme nervousness, headache, arthritis, neuritis, gastric and intestinal indigestion, weakness and prostration, irritating vaginal discharge, palpitation of the heart, shortness of breath.

The cessation of vicarious elimination through the womb may bring a still more disastrous result. When the exit gate is closed by the menopause, the toxins continue to move in the direction of the womb and infiltrate it. Inflammation gradually increases. Eventually a watery discharge with a characteristic metallic odor may begin to ooze from the lymphatic vessels of the womb. This could be a first warning of uterine cancer.

During menstruation there are often symptoms in the breast, such as tingling, pain, or swelling of the milk glands. There is no doubt that the breast glands are mildly stimulated by the increased amount of ovarian hormone in the general blood circulation. If the woman is normal and not toxic, a few drops of milk may be secreted. But if she is toxic, Nature often forces some of the toxic material out through the milk glands, resulting in pain, soreness, and swelling. If the secretion is corrosive, it may cause an inflammation which can obstruct the excretory ducts. The milk gland may swell and become filled with toxic milk, resulting in a cyst, usually a half inch to an inch and a half in diameter. It is however an exceedingly simple procedure for the doctor to insert a needle into this cyst and aspirate the contents. Its color may be clear, milky, or stained with green or black bile. It is disagreeably metallic to the taste.

After the menopause, when periodic breast inflammation no longer occurs, a slow, steady vicarious elimination may concentrate in the glandular tissues of the breast and result in the growth of a cancer. In women, the highest percentage of cancer development occurs between 40 and 60 years of age, usually after the menopause, although it may arise at an earlier age if the toxemia is severe or if vicarious elimination is interrupted.

As the rising concentration of toxins hastens the onset of disease, the liver and kidneys are greatly damaged by forced efforts to clear the bloodstream. A fatal prognosis, then, for most cancer sufferers, would stem from the inability of the liver and kidneys to rally even with the best of therapeutic support. It is to be hoped that there will come a time when, after careful study has been made of the patient's body chemistry, diet chemistry, glandular heredity and kidney-liver function, the prospective cancer case can be taught to correct her chemical mistakes and thereby avoid becoming a victim of this disease.

For the patient suffering from milder disturbances of menstruation and menopause, much relief can be offered.

The painful period may be relieved by reducing the concentration of toxins in the blood. This is best accomplished by limiting the diet for one or two days just before the period begins. Urine tests will indicate whether the toxins are protein, or starch-and-sugar-related. If the latter, then the appropriate antidote is an acidic cleanser consisting of diluted fruit juices taken every hour. If protein acids are the offenders, an alkalinic base, such as diluted raw vegetable juice, yeast, or vegetable soup (without meat) is prescribed. No other food should be taken for this day or two. As the blood toxemia is reduced, the urine becomes less acid and lighter in color. Therefore, frequent checks of the urine provide valuable criteria to indicate how long the limited diet may be necessary. As the blood clears, the endocrine glands function more normally.

The increase in thyroid activity during menstruation hastens elimination through the outer skin, often giving rise to offensive body odors. This makes bathing imperative. One or more rather warm baths should be taken daily. The old idea that a woman should not bathe during menstruation is as obsolete as the belief that night air is bad to breathe. However, it is wiser not to swim or take cold baths during the period inasmuch as the shock of cold water will sometimes stop the flow.

Even more important is cleanliness of the inner skin. There may be offensive odors at this time from the mouth, teeth, and tongue. Likewise, the more irritating and odorus the vaginal discharges, the more imperative is vaginal hygiene. For example, douching with water when needed can be helpful.

To the woman suffering menopausal difficulties a simple, wholesome diet is very helpful, along with periods of rest, catnaps in the afternoon if she is home, or periods of rest on weekends if she works. During this time of change in a woman's life I recommend a diet plentiful in green alkaline vegetables. Small amounts of proteins are also good: eggs, rare lamb, beef, chicken, or fish. Fruits, such as apples, bananas, and Babcock peaches in season, are excellent for natural sugar. Some women enjoy herb tea with honey around 4 o'clock.

Sometimes my patients find it beneficial to start creative hobbies such as oil painting, needlework, or macrame. One lady I know is learning to make jewelry. Keeping the mind active will prove beneficial.

I find that to numerous women approaching middle age the menopause is frightening, as with the housewife from Canada. This patient's complaints were many. First, she was exuding a bilious yellow perspiration on her chest. She was also growing a coarse beard and her cranial hair was falling out. Her voice had become masculine and gravelly. She told me that at this point in her life she just wanted to crawl away somewhere and hide.

My first examination revealed liver impairment. I told her it might take two years before we would see any improvement. I put her on a regime of vegetable broth, rare beef or lamb once daily, and as much zucchini squash, string beans, lettuce, celery, and cucumbers as she could eat. I also prescribed small amounts of estrogen hormones.

A few months later, I received a letter describing her physical changes as she followed the diet. She wrote:

> Apart from the reduction of pain, as I progressed on the diet, there was a gradual tissue change starting at the neck. I was just fifty years old, weighed 149 pounds, and stood five feet, four inches tall. Gradually the flesh on my upper body lost its former puffiness. I became thinner; even my legs, which were heavy all of my life, and I saw that I had ankle bones for the first time. I lost my gravel voice. My hair came in plentifully and even filled in areas which had become thin over the years.
>
> My energy increased sufficiently to allow me to swim two or three times a week. I went to Yoga classes.
>
> My eyes became clear and bright, my nails improved. And best of all, I had, for the first time in my life, a spot-free complexion which had a nice closed-pore texture to it. I suddenly became very interesting to my professional friends and close social contacts. My personal life became more exciting than ever before. Everyone wanted to know how I had done it, my male friends told me I looked

fifteen years younger. Psychologically I was greatly improved and regained my sense of humor and mental alertness.

On this diet I find that I am odorless, my mouth tastes fresh, there is a lightness, a general clean feeling that I have never experienced before.

Sometimes my women patients suffer from anxieties and depressions because of lifelong habits of eating foodless food and drinking large amounts of toxic stimulants. A few years ago, a spiritual practicioner came to me for an examination. She was undergoing extreme mental anguish and unbearable physical suffering during her menopause. In addition to hot flashes, she had shingles, constipation, and inflammation of a large vein in her left leg. She had damaged her liver so badly, by dietary indiscretions, I didn't know if I could help her, and I told her so.

She was a woman of great faith and replied that to get well she would rigidly maintain whatever diet I advised. I put her on zucchini squash only; she was to eat it every two hours.

Six months later, after a series of bile crises, her liver had improved. Her shingles were better, and her other problems less severe. I began to add one food at a time to her zucchini diet, until she was well.

Two years later, her liver had repaired itself. Her hot flashes were gone, along with her other symptoms; she was free to continue her studies and to help others.

Once in a while, I find it necessary to prescribe estrogen in minute amounts, if I notice during my examination symptoms of hormone imbalance. I carefully supervise the amounts of estrogen taken, along with the diets. The hormone balance of the body is very delicate, and harm to the patient may occur with indiscriminate use.

With a simple wholesome diet, a good mental attitude, work and hobbies balanced with rest, and preferably some male companionship, today's woman will find herself stepping into a new cycle of freedom. Free from toxic menstruation each month, she can look forward to a symptomless menopause, good health, and a fulfilling sex life throughout all the years to come.

MASTURBATION 16

Masturbation is the act of handling one's own genitals, or the genitals of another, for sexual gratification. Masturbation is most intense during the teenage period of both boys and girls due to the hormonal changes that occur. These changes drive many adolescents to masturbation for release of inner pressures they can no longer hold in check. We must remember that the newly awakened sex drive, and its attendant rise in sex energy, is Nature's way of preparing teenagers for procreation within a few years.

As a general rule, boys are more active than girls during the teen years. The sexual pressure that builds up in teenage boys is tremendous, with hormones pouring into their bloodstream.

This is a period of preoccupation with sex. For the first time, orgasms occur. Until now, masturbation has been primarily self-fondling with pleasant sensations.

In boys the first orgasms are dry, no seminal fluid, no sperm. Later, fluids appear, and still later, sperm in increasing amounts.

Girls also begin to feel real genital titillation for the first time. Erection of the clitoris and engorgement of the labia minora induce attention to the sexual organs.

With both boys and girls around 13 years of age, masturbation acts as a bridge, helping to make the transition to heterosexuality. It can play a part too in precluding the possibility of premature pregnancy, releasing sexual tensions either hormonally or toxically induced. Masturbation is the sexual act which, so to speak, "tries out" the sexual equipment. Recognition that sexual stimulation is a process that proceeds to orgasm is established.

The term masturbation comes from the Latin word *masturbari*, "to pollute oneself."

This is a good definition when related to inner pollution caused by eating foods high in salt content—dill pickels, french fried potatoes, any foods with a heavy concentration of salt—which can be responsible for toxic masturbation.

The toxic masturbation prevalent during the puberty period, in both boys and girls, is very often due to the toxic concentrations of salt, white sugar, and other irritants that may have been building up since babyhood.

While masturbation merely due to growth toward adulthood has always existed and served a useful purpose as a natural release, I have seen damage done to the prostate gland in the male, and the womb in the female, from frustrated acts of unnatural masturbation. Unnatural masturbation is instigated by toxic poisons being eliminated through the prostate and womb, the irritations of these poisons causing forced and excessive manipulation of the penis or clitoris.

There are those teenagers who feel forced to masturbate three and four times a day in an attempt to free themselves of the scratchy, burning, itchy sensations. Such masturbation actually can inflame or even damage their sex glands. Change the dietary habits of these young people so that their livers and kidneys are restored to their natural functions, and the toxic secretions will stop within six months to a year.

The case history of a 17-year-old male patient vividly illustrates what happens when guilt about (toxic) masturbation causes problems that upset, psychologically and physically, the life of a teenager.

My patient began to masturbate when he was 7 years old. His grandfather caught him in the act on more than one occasion and told him his penis would shrivel up and fall off if he didn't stop.

His family were heavy pork-eaters. They had bacon, sausage, or ham every morning for breakfast. Ham and pork chops were regularly on their dinner menu. They were also addicted to heavy starches and used vinegar, salt, and spices generously. The boy's liver and kidneys thus deleteriously affected at an early age by salt poisoning, he found himself driven to masturbate sometimes five to seven times daily, despite a latent fear stemming from his grandfather's warning.

By age 17, the burden of guilt—double guilt, actually—had become unbearable. When he compared his penis to those of other boys in the gym showers, he saw that his was smaller than most and was convinced his had shrunk and would continue to shrink if he didn't stop masturbating.

I explained that it was impossible for his penis to shrink. We uncovered his grandfather's warning as the deep-rooted cause of part of his guilt feelings. I told him what had happened to his liver and kidneys, how they had been harmed as a direct result of his earlier food habits and that his prostate was striving to eliminate years of accumulated poison.

I prescribed a simple diet and recommended that he participate in more sports. Because he was young and followed his diet, a year later the compulsion to masturbate because of toxic pressure had stopped. Today he is happily married and has a son of his own whom he has taught to understand the role of proper food to good sexual health.

In the book *Patterns of Sexual Behavior,* by Clellan S. Ford and Frank A. Beach, the authors cite the Kinsey, Pomeroy, and Martin report as stating that 92 percent of American men masturbate to the point of orgasm at least once during their lifetime. Estimates by various other researchers indicate that the same statement may be made about 85 to 96 percent of males in European countries. The Kinsey team reported that 69 percent of American husbands who are college graduates masturbate at least occasionally. It has also been established that genital self-stimulation tends to increase in men during their sixties.

American youth who masturbate and then stop the practice usually do so because self-stimulation is replaced by heterosexual intercourse.

Ford and Beach further cite a sampling taken of 295 American women, which showed that 54 percent of them had masturbated at one time or another. One quarter of these women practiced the habit at least once a week during the time when they were masturbating, and 25 percent of these had indulged in such self-stimulation regularly. The majority of masturbators had begun the practice early in life but, after adolescence when heterosexual interests became predominant, tended to drop the habit. It was also found that 74 percent of one group of married women had some masturbatory experience, the habit being almost universal in widows past 40. A survey of 1,183 unmarried women with a college education showed that two thirds had masturbated at some time, although many had never reached orgasm in this way. One third of those who masturbated stopped within one year after beginning; one half continued for ten to twenty years.

Among those women who eventually ceased to masturbate, several reasons were given for discontinuing, the most common being fear of physical and mental deterioration. This applied to women who both had and had not achieved orgasm through self-stimulation. Among women who had thus reached orgasm, the second most common reason given for discontinuance was that feelings of shame and disgust resulted from self-manipulation.

These feelings of shame and disgust were engendered, in my opinion, by conditioned parents who themselves felt shameful and guilty about sex matters.

I have found that many women masturbate out of a desire to rid themselves of toxic sexual secretions that irritate the womb, vagina, and clitoris. This form of masturbation can cause intense pain, as well as temporary relief, to the female's genitalia.

One such young woman patient of mine had caused a red, raw area to appear around her clitoris. She found it painful to walk because of a constant irritation resulting from leukorrhea, an abnormal whitish-yellowish discharge. Her urinalysis and background history showed that there was sugar damage to the liver. Because of the malfunctioning liver, her vagina was being used as an avenue of vicarious elimination.

Food therapy for this woman consisted of large amounts of alkaline vegetables and small amounts of proteins. Whole grain cereal was the only starch I allowed. I also recommended that she stay in bed until the discharge stopped and the tender skin around her clitoris healed.

Six weeks later her condition had cleared. As this experience was not one she wished ever to recur, she has faithfully adhered to the diet.

Looking overall at the matter of masturbation, I feel it to be fortunate that the population in general has had some of the veils of ignorance about this and other sexual matters lifted. Masturbation should be recognized as a safety valve to some and as a secondarily acceptable (and perhaps temporary) sex substitute to others. Masturbation, as we have seen, is not always prompted by Nature's preparation to indulge in adult sex; it can be due to a toxic condition, and when this is the case then it can be harmful. And the toxic condition should be corrected.

THE
MALE MENOPAUSE

17

Just like the female, all males go through a change of life. However, their change is more gradual, more difficult to diagnose and therefore to treat.

In the female the disappearance of menstrual periods, the beginning of hot flashes, the emotional mood swings, are unmistakable indications that menopause has started.

In the male different physical and psychological manifestations occur.

On the psychological level there is the growing fear of aging and, likely because of ignorance, the additional fear of losing the ability to have an erection.

Not too many men are aware of Masters and Johnson's statement, in their book *Human Sexual Inadequacy:* "With effective dissemination of information by proper authority, the aging man can be expected to continue in a sexually effective manner into his ninth decade."

Though few men in this country live past the age of 90, it is safe to say that the male is capable of enjoying sex until the day he dies. The aging male should understand the natural involutional changes that invariably develop in the established pattern of sexual performance.

One of the first problem signs of the onset of the male menopause is worry about getting an erection. According to Masters and Johnson older males should realize that it takes a little longer to obtain an erection than when they were younger. But once achieved, their erections, as a rule, last longer. This is due to a longer "response cycle" with advanced age.

It is necessary for some aging males to use a sex-steroid testosterone replacement to help increase his sex drive. The male hormone testosterone is given orally in pill form or injected, to help obtain and subsequently maintain an erection.

A few years ago, I had a 58-year-old teacher come to me. He was a pituitary type, tall and distinguished-looking. His main complaints were an insatiable yet unfulfilling sex urge, blurring vision, and deafness in both ears. Many previous examinations by specialists failed to reveal the cause of his eye and ear problems, which were becoming increasingly serious.

He had been raised on foods that contained a very heavy content of salt. From an early age he had drank coffee in large amounts. Moreover, he started smoking cigarettes when quite young, and now smoked two to three packs a day, thus adding to his general toxicity. He had been leaning heavily on coffee and cigarette stimulation to get him through the day and to provide him with false energy to indulge in heavy sexual activity at night. He didn't realize the damage he was doing to his adrenal glands, which in turn were causing the serious eye and ear condition and the blurring vision.

I prescribed a diet of whole-grain cereal and two soft-cooked egg yolks for breakfast; rare lamb, beef, broiled chicken, or fish, cooked vegetables, and a salad of cucumbers, celery, and butter lettuce, with salad dressing made of olive oil and vinegar for lunch.

He was also to have a glass of fruit juice, such as grape or apple, mixed with an equal amount of water at midmorning and mid-afternoon. A banana around 4 o'clock; and repeat his lunch at dinner. I cut down his coffee and cigarette intake gradually, so that he wouldn't have any withdrawal problems. In time he was able to give them up altogether.

On a second visit six weeks later, he reported that his eyesight had improved. He asked me if there was anything he could do about his sex life, which seemed unnatural to him at this stage of his life because of its intensity and lack of fulfillment. I told him he was a highly sexed pituitary type, driven by strong, uncontrollable drives to have intercourse, and that he felt empty and unfulfilled afterwards because his sex was a mere physical act separated from love or affection. I explained that he was using sex to rid himself of the salt in his system. By copulation he was eliminating the salt toxicant through his genitals, together with his seminal discharge.

After he had been three months on the simple salt-free diet I recommended, his sex drive normalized; the act became more enjoyable, with pleasurable feeling in his genitals. He became relaxed and less driven in his search for fulfillment.

Three months later his hearing had returned to normal, along with improved vision.

Inner pollution causes premature aging in the male. Salt toxemia gives a dry, parched look and early wrinkles to the skin, the skin loses its elasticity. Hair turns gray earlier, or falls out from lack of circulation. Far too many men are bald by the time they reach 30. These are problems that can so often be prevented, or, in any event, the pace of aging can be decelerated.

Nature insists upon three physical laws for humans, particularly those whose health is not ideal: rest, nutrition, and exercise. All must be obeyed. About the age of 40 the cells of the testicle, which secrete the male hormones, become less vigorous—begin to slow down. Testosterone, the only male sex hormone, is primarily secreted by the testicles, a secondary source being the adrenal glands. A few drops a day of this hormone help keep a man muscular, and his internal sexual structures, the seminal vesicles and the testicles, in functioning order. Very gradually as the output of testosterone diminishes, male sexuality lessens. At this point many men begin to have a fear—a dread in some cases—about their future maleness. It is then that some are driven to overcompensate by seeking increased sexual activity.

It is of course wise to have periodic medical examinations during the advancing years. If the system is not toxic, then it is reasonable to expect that a good life, including a good sex life, can be continually enjoyed. If there is concern about orgasm and/or sex on the part of the patient, the doctor most probably will do a urinary gonadotropin test. This test will show if the patient needs reinforcement of testosterone.

Frequently I have found that, with a food therapy plan which cleanses the body and restores it to normal function, testosterone is not necessary or can soon be eliminated. I carefully watch the patient's progress, the way he acts and reacts to his sexual problems or experiences, before I prescribe anything further.

When the body is in chemical balance, and the male secure in his ability to function in all areas of his life, then there is no need for him to fear menopause.

"RESPECTABLE" DRUGS AND YOU 18

"Respectable" drugs are those found in a large percentage of medicine cabinets across the country.

These are the mood-altering, or mind-affecting, psychotropic—sometimes regarded as affecting the sex centers of the brain—drugs with which respectable, middle-class men and women are increasingly "turning on." Usually these drugs are obtained by prescription; often they are not. You would recognize many of their names.

We can categorize these drugs in five groups. The first group is the Relaxants. They are designed to reduce anxiety. It is exceedingly unwise to take these if there is alcohol in the system.

The second group is Major Tranquilizers. They can modify psychotic symptoms and can reduce fear and hostility. They may be potentially addictive, and can prove very dangerous in combination with alcohol or sedatives.

The third group is comprised of Antidepressants or mood elevators. They alleviate serious depression. They can also interact dangerously with alcohol, amphetamines, sedatives, and a number of other substances. Side effects often include blurred vision and dizziness.

The fourth group consists of Amphetamines. These pills stimulate the central nervous system, thus preventing fatigue and creating a sense of confidence. However, high doses may cause toxic psychosis. Abuse can produce psychic dependence and possible addiction.

The fifth group is the Barbiturates. This group affects the central nervous system. They are depressants that sedate (calm) or, in larger doses, induce sleep. They can also cause psychic dependence. If abused, their use may lead to addiction.

The word *abuse* means to ingest in excess of prescribed dosage and/or duration of time.

A San Francisco General Hospital team of physicians, headed by Dr. David E. Smith, reported recently that in the field of barbiturates (sleeping pills) alone, "approximately 300 tons . . . are consumed in the United States per year, and barbiturate abuse has become a major health problem in this country."

That respectable drugs can be as harmful as those that are illegal may be witnessed by this case from my files concerning a top-paid model who was a victim of respectable drugs—sleeping pills, diet pills, tranquilizers, and painkillers.

When this young woman came to me she was completely disoriented and lethargic. She had collapsed during a photographic session. Her friends, patients of mine, feared for her life and had recommended that she see me. She was pale and pasty; black-and-blue marks covered her arms and legs; her equilibrium had been disturbed.

She had started her career as a teenage model and began to gain weight from a heavy intake of soft drinks, ice cream, starches, and candy bars. It was at this time that her mother took her to a doctor renowned for his ability to help overweight people reduce. With the aid of this doctor—and the drugs he prescribed, including amphetamines—she was able to reduce from 150 to 110 pounds which, for her 5 foot 8 inch frame, was underweight.

Most weight-reduction pills are amphetamines, the so-called pep pills. Continued use of these causes abnormal stimulation and excitability which dangerously mask fatigue. What actually happens is that the body is in fact fatigued while the brain continues to signal action to which the body can no longer properly respond. The false feeling of well-being is thus invariably followed by severe depression as the effect of the pep pills wears off.

Fearful that she would gain back the poundage, she continued to take diet pills after losing weight. She drank ten cups of black coffee a day, ate grapefruit and hard-boiled eggs and not much else. The overstimulation from coffee acids and pep pills made for sleeplessness at night. She then turned to sleeping pills. After a while the ever-increasing dosages of sleeping pills no longer worked. Now she found that by drinking two glasses of vodka mixed with orange juice, plus a couple of sleeping pills, sleep could be induced.

It was at this time that the physical sense of depression resulting from the toxemia in her bloodstream, together with an accompanying sense of alienation and aloneness, caused her to reach out for love from men she met casually at work or at social affairs after work.

In her state of muddled thinking and emotions, plus a physically exhausted body, she responded poorly to sex. She had no feeling during intercourse, which further depressed her. Her liver and kidneys—all her avenues of vicarious elimination, including her female organs—were working overtime to eliminate the heavy load of toxins from her system.

Her nerves became painfully taut. Guilt about her sexual promiscuity made her irritable and snappy with co-workers; she lost modeling assignments. She suffered migraine headaches. Her doctor then prescribed pain pills for the headaches. She would occasionally collapse and bruise herself.

Her first examination by me showed low blood pressure, anemia, a low red-blood count, malnutrition, and a highly disturbed emotional state.

I ordered her to bed, and gradually withdrew the pills, alcoholic beverages, and coffee. I gave her raw liver juice, large amounts of zucchini squash, string beans, cooked celery, green salads, cucumbers, raw egg yolks, and raw milk. As her system cleared, she left her bed and took walks in the sunshine.

Within the next two years, she began to glow with a renewed radiance of health. Her physical and emotional states were greatly improved. Her blood pressure was up to normal, and the anemia was gone. She was able to forgive herself for being promiscuous and found new meaning and true feeling in a relationship with a man who offered companionship on many levels.

Unhappily, some women do not survive drug abuse as fortunately as did my model-patient.

The following is an account of twin brothers, the only children of middle-class parents, who were reared in the Midwest in comfortable surroundings. In fact, they were as removed from any sophisticated drug-oriented culture as two children could be. Both attended college. One became a lawyer and the other a research librarian.

The lawyer moved to California and the librarian went East. After his ten-year marriage ended in divorce, the lawyer developed a duodenal ulcer that necessitated an operation for removal of two thirds of his stomach. During the postoperative period he gained considerable weight. He went to a doctor for help, began taking pills of different kinds, and became addicted. He lost weight but became so stimulated he couldn't sleep. He was then given tranquilizers and sleeping pills which he took, sometimes both at the same time, because he still had difficulty sleeping. His tolerance level was built up to the point where he needed twice the original dosage to put him to sleep.

When intense migraine headaches started, he was given a prescription for painkillers. He was now taking all of the above-mentioned drugs together.

He lost consciousness one day, fell, and suffered a concussion. His brother was called to come help to take care of him. The librarian pleaded with his brother to stop taking drugs. But the lawyer was so addicted he couldn't stop. Three times he was arrested for drunk driving, yet none of the times was there a sufficiently high level of alcohol in his blood to sustain the charge. Actually the drugs, and not the drink or two of alcohol he'd had, were responsible for his erratic driving.

Once, in a period of deep depression, he attempted suicide. His brother tried to convince him to commit himself to an institution where he could try to be freed of the addiction, but the lawyer refused to admit he was addicted. He suffered another fall and was unconscious for hours before his brother found him. He was rushed to the hospital where he died a few hours later from a blood clot on the brain.

Female Dependency on Drugs

It is a commentary of our times that working women, who comprise 37.5 percent of the U.S. labor force, show an habitual dependency on drugs of one kind or another. Here is the percentage breakdown of the eight drugs most ingested by the female workers: nonbarbiturate sedatives, 44; major tranquilizers, 52; controlled narcotics, 53; relaxants, 62; amphetamines, 63; antidepressants, 67; and diet pills, 73.

According to a 1971 survey by Carl D. Chambers, Ph.D., Director of Research for the New York State Narcotic Addiction Control Commission, the working woman is 15 percent likelier to take barbiturates or diet pills than the non-working woman; over 20 percent more inclined to use relaxants; 33 percent likelier to take pep pills; 50 percent likelier to use a non-controlled narcotic; twice as likely to use one of the controlled drugs (opiates); and four times as likely to rely on one of the major tranquilizers. The following table gives a comparison of percentage drug use among all working women, working women with college degrees, and house-wives.

Types of Drugs Used	All Working Women	Working Women with College Degrees	Housewives
		(percentages)	
Relaxants	15	20	13
Non-controlled narcotics	14	17	9
Barbiturates	8	6	7
Marijuana	8	14	1
Diet pills	7	7	6
Non-barbiturate sedatives	5	7	5
Amphetamines	2	5	1.5
Controlled narcotics	2	3	1
Major tranquilizers	2	1	0.5
Antidepressants	1	2	2

College students and college graduates depend more on marijuana and hashish and the amphetamine family than do housewives or working women. Men who are in college or who are college graduates smoke marijuana and hashish and use LSD more than the middle-class white-collar worker.

Many doctors used to think that only half a dozen narcotics, including heroin and morphine, could cause true addiction and that the victim could give up other drugs without suffering withdrawal. It has been discovered, however, that there are many non-narcotic drugs that can lead to addiction, with consequent withdrawal agonies when an attempt is made to desist. Long-term use of barbiturates can addict. So can the minor tranquilizers, and the amphetamines.

How do people get started taking these "respectable" drugs? I will say that anyone brought up on a clean diet, or who has adopted a clean diet, most generally will have a body that is in a state of vibrant health. Such a person does not therefore have the craving for, or need of, artificial stimulation—like the false pep from pep pills, chemical tranquilizers, or muscle relaxants—to set him at peace with himself. He is already at peace. His brain is not being flooded with toxins to stir him up or to depress him.

Marijuana, hashish, and LSD are supposed to heighten feeling in the sexual experience. Males and females who are sexually healthy already have sufficiently sensitive genitals. They do not require the artificial stimulation of either the respectable or illegal drugs which so often cause vital organ malfunction and destruction.

Any decision to change from deleterious or hazardous eating and drug-taking habit patterns should be done under a doctor's supervision. His experience and care is necessary to supervise and help control the withdrawal symptoms as toxic drugs are eliminated from the system.

It would be well for anyone taking drugs of any kind to consider cleansing his or her body. Once the decision is made to do so and the transformation is completed to good health— *natural* good health—greater body sensitivity will be evidenced and vibrant enjoyment of life will be possible.

PART III:

THE BEST
IN FOODS

FOOD IS YOUR
BEST APHRODISIAC 19

Aphrodisiacs of one kind or another have existed since time immemorial. (The term *aphrodisiac* derives from the name of the ancient Greek goddess of love, Aphrodite.)

An aphrodisiac is a drug—or any other agent— used to increase sexual fervor. Spanish fly is a classic example. It is made from small beetles found in southern France and in Spain. These insects are dried and pulverized, then treated chemically to extract a drug called *cantharidin*. When a few drops of Spanish fly (cantharidin) are imbibed by a woman, she is supposed to become aroused almost instantly. What actually happens is that her adrenals become over-stimulated, and she may just as easily go into convulsions as become passionate. This drug is also a bladder irritant; when excreted in the urine it burns the lining of the bladder and urethra, and may reflexly stimulate the sexual organs. The male who takes the drug may get a painful erection which may—or may not—climax in an orgasm.

Orientals used to swear by powdered rhinoceros horn,

which was supposed to improve male potency. Another, more modern Oriental remedy is ginseng root, ginseng powder, or ginseng tea. In any form, ginseng promotes artificial adrenal stimulation—and sometimes adrenal exhaustion.

During the Victorian era, men who were having sexual difficulties were given "prairie oysters," a polite term for bull's testicles. These were supposed to be eaten absolutely fresh and raw, the theory being that they contained male hormone. Unfortunately for the theory, most of the hormone would be destroyed by gastric juices before it could achieve its effect.

A drug called yohimbine, made from the inner bark of the African yohimbine tree, has been used countless times as an aphrodisiac, and somehow never works.

The efficacy of these unusual aphrodisiacs seems to exist solely in the credence that desperate or curious people give to them.

However, there are some aphrodisiacs that may just be helpful—and not myth-based. Oysters, for example, are considered an aphrodisiac. From the standpoint of sexual health, oysters *do* add minerals, especially calcium, to the total dietary picture. Clams also contribute to sexual health, since they contain iodine, minerals, and calcium.

I usually recommend raw egg yolks as a food aphrodisiac to rebuild exhausted adrenals. With adrenal depletion, there can be no adequate supply of sexual energy.

Avocados are another food aphrodisiac. They contain vitamin E, which is beneficial to the sex glands.

Actually, a balanced wholesome food diet—containing proteins in small amounts, natural starches, sugars, fats, balanced with cooked and raw vegetables and fresh fruit—may not be exotic, mysterious, expensive, or difficult to find, but is an aphrodisiac that works.

EATING
IN RESTAURANTS 20

A first-class restaurant is a social gathering place, a place where families enjoy togetherness, where lovers often begin and end romances, where old friends meet to share memories of past experiences, and where new friends meet to begin new experiences.

There are two ways of eating intelligently in a restaurant. The first is to bring your own vegetables and have the chef prepare them to order, which is what I do on occasion. Admittedly, this is a difficult thing to manage. The second requires that you make it clear to your waiter or waitress that you want little or no salt added to your meat, vegetables, potatoes, or salad. This request should be fulfilled in a first-class restaurant.

Steak house restaurants usually feature prime rib or different cuts of quality steaks. There is natural salt in this meat and it does not require additional salting, or sauce. The less seasoning on steak the better. The same applies to lamb and chicken.

Here is a sample of courses to follow when you dine at a steak house: Begin with salad, with oil and vinegar dressing, and one or two cooked vegetables. The meat entre can be rare prime rib, steak, broiled lamb chops, or chicken. Boiled potatoes are desirable, if available, or freshly done mashed potatoes (not those from a "prepared mix"). Whole grain or rye bread is preferred, with butter. For dessert, have fresh fruit in season. If you feel you must drink an alcoholic beverage, limit it to one drink, two at the most. Black coffee or tea should not surpass one cup, especially at night.

In a seafood restaurant, fish such as halibut, sole, or red snapper should be broiled, not fried in bread crumbs. Oysters, crabs, clams, shrimp, and lobster should be broiled, boiled, or eaten raw. Potatoes, boiled or mashed, rice, cooked vegetables, and salad will make for a satisfying meal. Since liquids dilute the digestive juices, I do not drink beverages of any kind with a meal. However, if you must, the same rule applies for beverages as in the steak-house menu: moderation.

Italian restaurants usually feature pasta in one form or another, a food that should be eaten only in small amounts. These restaurants usually have excellent salads, with olive oil and vinegar dressings. The better Italian restaurants feature steaks, broiled chicken, and fish. They also serve zucchini (excellent for the system) and tomato dishes to balance the amount of starch. If wine is ordered, it should be in small amounts. If you feel you must have a dessert, select fresh fruit.

Before ordering in a Chinese restaurant, check with the chef and make sure that the food is not prepared with monosodium glutamate. Eat Chinese food in small amounts. Rice is excellent. However, Chinese tea, like coffee, should be consumed in moderation, if at all.

Japanese restaurants usually feature raw fish, and rice, which is excellent if not drowned in soy sauce. Cooked dishes should not contain monosodium glutamate.

A healthy rule to follow when at a restaurant is to eat in moderation, and take plenty of time between servings. Consider going to a restaurant as a form of entertainment or a meeting place, not as an excuse to deviate from healthful eating habits.

OPTIMUM FOOD LISTS 21

Optimum foods are, as the dictionary states, the best or most favorable foods. In setting up optimum food lists—or any type of food lists, for that matter—it must be kept in mind that the foods we eat are comprised basically of proteins, starches, fats, and (natural) sugar. When selecting foods for my optimum list, which follows in this chapter, I have also taken into consideration the three body types.

Since what I may note as optimum may not in all instances be accepted as such by others, I am offering as well a "twilight-zone" list. The toxic food list which I present is, of course, to be recognized as a "don't touch" reminder to everyone who wishes to have good health.

In the protein family, the best way to cook meat is to broil it lightly or have it boiled. Eggs should be eaten raw, soft-cooked, or poached. I recommend raw cow's milk or goat's milk for their quality. Pecans are a fine source of vegetable protein and are eaten raw, always in small amounts, and masticated thoroughly, as they are highly concentrated. Fish, sea food, and chicken should be boiled, never covered in bread crumbs and fried in grease.

206

In the starch family, wheat is excellent in the whole grain breads, if you wish to add weight. Rye bread builds muscle. It is best to make your own bread if you can find time. I use the small red potatoes and boil them. I never recommend baked potatoes, because baking changes the potato's chemistry into something resembling laundry starch. Frying potatoes in grease, especially when adding salt, creates a toxic combination that is hard on the digestion. I find that whole grain cereal is alkaline and has very little starch. Oatmeal and wheat-germ cereals are also excellent. I consider bananas to be one of the finest natural starch foods available. They are rich in potassium and should be eaten ripe.

I advise that natural sugars be taken only in small amounts. Honey should be raw and not filtered. Pure maple syrup, molasses, or raw sugar is allowed.

Fats, like sugars, must be used sparingly. Unsalted butter, raw cream, avocado, apricot kernel oil, or olive oil sprinkled on salads are excellent.

I either steam my cooked vegetables or cook them in a pressure cooker. If I am cooking zucchini squash, string beans, Chinese pea pods, Chinese cabbage, corn, or chard and beet tops, I time them for four to seven minutes from the moment the steam is in operation. Then I shut them off. Many times I combine two or more vegetables for flavor. Sometimes, because of the season, when I am unable to find fresh vegetables, I use frozen vegetables whose labels show that no chemicals have been involved in their preparation.

I usually eat my raw vegetables plain. Many of my patients prefer to make salads.

Fruits are a wonderful source of natural sugar, vitamins, minerals, and pure water. They are eaten raw, perhaps with the exception of Rome Beauty apples, which may be baked. Fruits are best eaten between meals, usually one piece of fruit of any kind at a time—I use frozen blueberries (no sugar added), topped with raw cream. I also recommend that fruits should be eaten in season. Herb tea, with or without a teaspoon of raw honey, makes an enjoyable hot or cold beverage. Peppermint, alfalfa mint, rosehips, comfrey, chamomile, linden flowers, and parsley teas are all delightful. For cold beverages, I give fruit juices diluted with equal parts of distilled water. They have a gentle cleansing effect on the body. These juices include apple, orange, pineapple, grape, grapefruit, guava, and papaya.

Often there is an adjustment period in changing from an old way of eating to a new, simple way. Many people complain of virtual withdrawal symptoms. However, a little discipline, it seems to me, is a small price to pay for vibrant health.

In the starch family, oatmeal in small amounts is permissable if it agrees with the individual. Spaghetti, macaroni, and noodles are highly concentrated starches and should be masticated thoroughly and eaten in very small amounts. If a short time after you have eaten you begin to burp, this is a strong indication that you are having difficulty digesting that particular food and should avoid it.

Many vegetables should be *tried* to determine which ones digest the best. Though most people consider them a vegetable, tomatoes, for instance, are really an acid fruit, containing much oxalic acid.

Artichokes, asparagus, yellow and green onions, watercress, and carrots should be tried for variety, but in small portions.

Deceptive Labelling and Food Additives

Since cola drinks contain caffeine they can be harmful. Dr. Samuel Bellet, Chief of Cardiology at Philadelphia General Hospital, has suggested that "caffeine may be more important than smoking in setting the stage for heart attacks." Certain persons, sensitive to caffeine, have reported markedly noticeable heart palpitations following a single cup of coffee or one bottle of cola. But how is the consumer to avoid bringing into the home something unwanted, perhaps deleterious, when its contents are not labeled?

One example of deceptive labeling practices occurred after

former Secretary of Health, Education and Welfare, Robert H. Finch, stated publicly that, for public-health safety reasons, he was ordering the artificial sweetener cyclamate removed from the market. Manufacturers of artificially sweetened jams, jellies, and fruits then obtained rulings that permitted them to add *either* saccharine or cyclamates to the products without identifying which sweetener was being used; they were allowed to merely label the product "artificially sweetened." Obviously it was impossible for the public to comply with the Finch warning when the presence of cyclamates was not distinctly identified on the labels of the many products in which it was used.

Disturbing questions have been raised about certain adverse effects of the additive MSG. One FDA official has stated privately to superiors that "like individuals who have adverse symptoms from eating other food items, the individuals who are susceptible to MSG should learn to stay away from food such as soups, with large amounts of MSG." But how is one to avoid monosodium glutamate when its presence in three major food categories—salad dressing, French dressing, and mayonnaise—is not labeled on their packages?

Dr. Roy Newton, vice-president in charge of research for Swift and Company, talked about what he called the "confusers." One of the "confusers" he cited ". . . is that table salt is poisonous under some conditions." To my mind, there is no doubt about large amounts of salt being injurious to the human system. Many others agree with me that food products are permitted on our store shelves that contain small amounts of chemical substances which, without being obvious to the consumer, can be highly injurious to his health when consumed over a long period of time. Often salt is included in foodstuffs without being listed.

When the hearings on Chemical Additives in Foods were held back in the 1950s, it was admitted that some 700 chemicals were being added to American foodstuffs. Grave doubt existed as to the safety of at least 150 of them. Since then, the total number of chemical additives in food has soared. Official estimates today reach up to 10,000. To list and describe fully all food and color additives that have received government sanction now requires a directory of five volumes, and there is no exact knowledge of the number in present use.

What harm can chemical food additives do? Some additives produce chemical changes in the food itself by altering its biological structure. Others produce disorders in the human system so insidious that they do not become apparent until long after the original exposure to the chemicals. Because of this, the additives may not even be suspected as the original instigators of trouble. The earliest signs of damage to vital organs may be indicated by microscopic changes that can be detected only by a trained pathologist.

Many chemical food additives interfere with the normal functioning of vitamins and enzymes, which work closely together in the body. Vitamins play an important role in releasing energy for all physiological processes, including cell repair. Closely associated with them are the enzymes, which are the effective agents of the whole life process. As long as each cell lives, it is continually being broken down and rebuilt. Energy is needed for this repair process. In a vitamin deficiency, where energy liberation is interfered with by the introduction of chemical food additives or other substances, the rebuilding process slows down or ceases; the cells die. When enough cells sicken and die, the body dies.

Injury or deterioration of the cells is recognized by physicians who are aware of vitamin and enzyme deficiency symptoms. Patients are easily fatigued, show such symptoms as weakness, constipation, loss of appetite, headache, disturbance of sleep, excessive irritability, depression, inability to concentrate, odd feelings in the fingers and toes, burning tongue, gas, and many other strange bodily sensations. These symptoms all too often may be classified vaguely as nervousness, neurasthenia, or imagination, when in reality they may stem from impairment of the vitamin-enzyme system of the body.

Medical authorities and researchers have suggested that losses or deficiencies of enzymes lead to many diseases. Commonly used chemical food additives, such as sulfur dioxide, sodium nitrate, food dyes, certain hormones used to stimulate plant and animal growth, antibiotics used in food production, fluorides used in processing water, and pesticides are all acknowledged enzyme destroyers.

According to medical researchers, adverse effects can occur even when the chemicals are present in exceedingly small amounts. For example, as little as 0.4 parts per million of DDT can inhibit a vital enzyme in human blood. Many chemical additives permitted in foods are present in amounts that adversely affect the body's enzymes.

Catalase is one important enzyme found almost universally in living cells, not only in human beings but also in animals, plants, and even in bacteria. This particular enzyme plays many vital roles. It is intimately related to cell respiration and buffers the cell from toxic substances, infection, virus, radiation, and cancer. The normal cell maintains a specific balance of catalase and hydrogen peroxide. Catalase controls the hydrogen peroxide at a very low level, converting it into oxygen and water. However, many · substances, including some chemical food additives, destroy catalase. When this happens the level of peroxide rises. In turn, there results in the electron-transport system of the cell a slowing down or stoppage. Cellular abnormalities may then develop and the cell becomes predisposed to tumor formation.

It is evident that if this fundamental biological mechanism is interfered with for a long enough time by physical and chemical agents present in our environment, whether in food, drink, or the air we breathe, then we shall see in peoples so exposed a progressive increase in the incidence of tumors. To help arrest this condition it is important to abolish some of the chemicals currently added to food and drink for preservation or coloring.

The ultimate would be to eliminate major toxins—such as salt, coffee, cigarettes, drugs (legal and illegal), alcohol—out of the human diet. However, to be realistic, this would cause a collapse in a way of life for a great many people, both figuratively and literally. This would certainly happen if they were asked to stop smoking suddenly, or to not have their morning coffee, or sleeping pills, or their pep pills and tranquilizers—the latter in some instances being used to produce a quieting effect from the extra pep derived from the pep pills. Which is another way of saying that some people would rather risk being sick than change.

However, there are people, young and old, who today want to live a life free of disease, bear healthy children, and enjoy family life.

How do I know this? It is a sign of the times. On my recent annual vacation tour from California to Colorado, up through Montana then back home, I noticed many hot dog and taco stands had closed. At the same time, I found health food businesses booming, with more and more people being attracted to this new way of life. Many supermarkets have added health food sections. More people are planting organic gardens, wherever they can find the space to do so. Increasingly, more women are baking their own bread and feeding their families simply, buying good, wholesome foods.

Now, with emphasis on wholesome foods that will, in my opinion, help you toward a healthy life and thus a fulfilling sex life, I offer my Optimum Food List. This and the other lists that follow suggest foods that are of Nature's finest quality. If used in a balanced diet, they will provide variety and the best in nourishment.

Optimum Food List

Proteins: Rare beef and lamb
Raw egg yolks
Raw milk
Pecans, almonds
Fish, sea food (boiled)
Chicken (boiled or broiled)

Starches: Whole grain bread (preferably make your own with no salt, little sweet, or shortening)
Boiled potatoes, rice
Cereal and grains
Bananas

Sugars: Raw sugar
Dark brown sugar
Maple sugar
Raw honey, molasses

Fats: Raw cream
Unsalted butter
Avocado
Apricot kernel oil
Olive oil

Vegetables:
  Cooked: Soft squashes
String beans (yellow and green)
Chinese peas
Potatoes
Chard and beet-tops
Fresh corn
Chinese cabbage

  Raw: Lettuce, celery, cucumbers
Alfalfa sprouts, water cress

Fruit: Apples, bananas
Babcock peaches, pears
Blueberries, oranges, grapefruit
Raspberries, watermelons
Cantaloupes
Papaya, grapes
Pineapple, cherries

Best Foods for Your Glands

Some of the foods I consider most helpful to normalize activity of the endocrine glands are included in the following list.

For the Adrenal Glands:
Raw egg yolks, fish, meat, raw milk

For the Gonads — Sex Glands:
Meat, eggs, fish, oatmeal, whole wheat bread and wheat germ, lentils, whole barley, liver, kidney beans, black molasses

For the Pituitary Gland:
Potatoes, lettuce, wheat germ, almonds, liver, agar-agar (a sea moss), raw egg yolks, parsley, meat, fish, raw milk

For the Parathyroid Glands:
Oranges, apples, cabbage, cucumber, lettuce, radishes, watercress, whole wheat, honey

For the Pancreas:
Eggs, milk, meat, fish, cabbage, lettuce

For the Thyroid Gland:
All sea food, particularly oysters, shrimps, and fresh salmon

Foods that I consider to be in the "twilight zone" are those that should be eaten in small amounts, if at all, and only when the person is in good health. The protein group of this category consists of cottage cheese and yogurt. Commercial cottage cheese has too much salt. Most commercial yogurt has synthetic lactic acid. Processed cheddar cheese and Swiss cheese—in fact almost all processed cheeses—are loaded with salt and preservatives. It always should be remembered that cheese is a decayed food, and should be eaten in small amounts if at all.

The third food category—the "don't touch" list—contains the toxic food poisoners, many of which have been emphasized throughout this book: white sugar, white-sugar products, white-flour products, soft drinks (dietetic as well as regular); in fact, any and all dead food that has been devitaminized and demineralized. What many people do not realize when shopping is that they sometimes buy a foodless food that contains potentially harmful hidden ingredients, not advertised on the product's label. So, buyer beware!

I have often been asked to suggest menus for the basic body types, and the following sample menus are therefore divided into the three categories—Adrenal, Thyroid, and Pituitary. These menus are for those individuals who are in good health.

As I mentioned earlier, the Adrenal person, male and female, has an excellent digestion and can well manage three good-sized meals a day, including a large breakfast. The following menus are suggested for the *Adrenal male.*

Breakfast

1 piece of cantaloupe or ½ grapefruit with 1 teaspoon of honey

2 poached eggs on two pieces of whole grain, buttered bread, or

1 cup of cooked whole grain cereal or oatmeal with ½ cup of raw milk. One teaspoon of unsalted butter may be added to the cereal

Lunch

1 6-ounce serving ground round of beef — broiled

1 large helping of cooked vegetables such as zucchini squash, string beans, cut wax beans, Italian beans, or 2 ears of corn-on-the-cob served with pat of unsalted butter, no salt

1 large helping of green salad with oil and lemon dressing

Midafternoon

1 piece of fruit in season

1 4-ounce glass of raw milk or hot herb tea with honey

Dinner

1 6-ounce serving of broiled fish

1 serving of cooked vegetables with 1 pat of butter (unsalted)

1 helping of cut up raw vegetables such as celery, cucumbers, green peppers, etc.

1 helping of broiled or mashed potatoes, or brown rice (1 piece of whole grain bread may be substituted).
1 piece of fruit or a small glass of milk is allowed

The *Adrenal woman* may want to cut down on the above-suggested portions. Common sense will help dictate the amounts of starch foods she may eat without gaining weight.

A sample menu for the *Thyroid male and female* is as follows. (Remember that the Thyroid type usually has a high metabolism, and I recommend that they eat five small meals a day.) Raw milk is important as they require extra calcium. They also need a little more starch than their Adrenal counterparts.

Breakfast

Whole grain cereal, with raw milk and butter

1 6-ounce glass of raw milk

Sometimes two raw egg yolks lightly whipped or blended into a glass of raw milk with 1 teaspoon of honey added, is enjoyed

Midmorning

1 ripe banana

Lunch

1 4-ounce serving of broiled lamb

1 piece of homemade bread, spread with butter

1 helping of cooked vegetables

Midafternoon

1 glass of raw or goat's milk

Dinner

1 piece of broiled chicken

2 ears of steamed corn-on-the cob

1 portion of cooked brown rice

1 small dinner salad with oil and vinegar dressing

If desired before bedtime, 1 glass of warm milk

The *Pituitary* individuals (male and female) particularly need to avoid salt or salty foods. They require large amounts of alkaline vegetables. Zucchini squash, string beans and celery are especially good for them, along with raw vegetables. The Pituitary female may desire to cut down on her portions of the following sample menus.

Breakfast

½ hour before breakfast, drink 1 glass of diluted fruit juice. Then follow with:

2 soft cooked eggs

1 piece of whole grain buttered bread

1 cup of hot herb tea if desired

Midmorning

1 glass of diluted fruit juice, or

1 piece of fruit

Lunch

1 or 2 pieces of cold broiled chicken breast

Large serving of cooked vegetables

1 boiled potato

1 serving of green salad made with either Romaine or butter lettuce, cucumbers, celery, and apricot or olive oil and vinegar dressing

Dinner

Bieler stew (found in the recipe section)

1 piece of whole grain buttered bread

1 salad

If hungry before bedtime, 1 piece of fruit, such as pear or apple

MY PERSONAL RECIPES

22

I eat very simply myself, so I do not require many recipes. But because of many requests from my patients for recipes, I began to experiment, test and enjoy my own concoctions.

Two of the recipes I consider to be remedies. The first, Bieler broth, is fine for cleansing the body of toxic wastes. It is tasty, and many patients who are enjoying good health have this soup for lunch or served with dinner.

The second remedy, liver juice, supplies fresh protein and iron, and helps to build the blood.

The first recipe I developed was for home-baked bread. I began baking my own bread to avoid eating the store-distributed brands that contained chemical preservatives. The aroma of bread baking in the oven, not to mention the taste of home-baked bread fresh from the pan, always gives me a lift.

Some of my more imaginative patients tell me that they have developed variations on some of my recipes and have enjoyed the results of their experimenting: For example, to name but one—substituting rye, soy, or bran flour for the 4 cups of unbleached white flour suggested in my bread recipe.

A number of the recipes that follow actually came from my patients. I was first introduced to Farina dumplings in Pasadena while lunching at the home of a patient. When I told her how much I had liked the dumplings, and that I was aware of how wholesome they were, she kindly gave me the recipe.

It pleases me that so many people of all ages these days are following the lead of the younger generation and are turning away from the unnatural, chemicalized foods and seeking out, in increasing numbers, foods that come directly from their natural habitats.

Here is the soup recipe which my patients refer to as Bieler Broth.

Bieler Broth

8 large zucchini squash, cut into short lengths
8 stalks celery, cut into 2-inch lengths
2 packages string beans, frozen or fresh equivalent
1 tablespoon unsalted butter
1 small handful cut-up parsely
1-1/2 cups (distilled) water

Cut ends off zucchini and place in a pressure cooker, together with celery, string beans, and water. Allow contents to cook for 10 minutes after steam begins. Place contents of cooker in a blender, add butter and parsley, blend, and eat. A thick broth may be obtained by mashing the contents of the cooker with only butter added.

For those who are feeling tired or run-down, or who are slightly anemic, the following remedy can be recommended.

Liver Juice

1/2 pound calf's liver, cut into 1/4 inch squares
1/2 cup distilled water

Put the liver and the water into a blender and blend at medium speed. Strain through a double layer of cheesecloth into a measuring cup or a glass jar. Refrigerate. Drink 4 ounces at a time every 4 hours. If desired, the recipe can be doubled, but it is best made fairly fresh, though the blend will keep for 24 hours.

Pepper Liver

1 pound calf's liver
2 tablespoons soy flour
2 large ripe tomatoes
1 yellow onion
1 green pepper
1 teaspoon garlic powder
1 small can dietetic tomato sauce (no salt added)

First slice liver into 1/4 inch strips; put two tablespoons of soy flour on a piece of paper toweling; then roll liver strips in soy flour and sprinkle lightly with garlic powder.

Slice onion thinly, tomatoes in small cubes, and the green pepper thinly, and then place these vegetables in a skillet that has been lightly oiled with soy or olive oil.

Cook on medium heat until onions and other vegetables are brown. Add liver and then brown it on both sides; turn heat down to simmer.

Add small can tomato sauce, cook for 20 to 25 minutes or until done.

This recipe provides six servings.

Home-made bread is another recipe favored by my patients. Here is my special recipe for bread.

Bieler Bread Recipe
(Milk Free — Salt Free)

4 cups white flour (unbleached)
2 cups whole wheat flour
Dash of cinnamon (if desired)
1 heaping tablespoon wheat grass cut into 1-1/4 lengths

Mix and stir well.

1 cup warm water
2 cakes active fresh or
    2 tablespoons active dry yeast
1 cup hot water
1 teaspoon apricot kernel oil or sweet butter
1 teaspoon honey

Mix the above with flour mixture, stir well with a wooden stick or spoon, and add more warm water to make a firm consistency. Cover bowl with a moist towel and allow to rise, doubling its size. Knead and let rise again. Shape into a long roll. Cut into 18 equal pieces and place in muffin tins. Allow to rise in a warm oven (temp. 99 degrees) until double in bulk. Bake at 400 degrees for 25 minutes; then lower heat to 350 degrees for 60 minutes.

You may mix your own flour combinations if you desire using rye, buckwheat, millet, potato, bran, cracked wheat, etc. It is best to keep proportions to two parts white to one part other flours. When extra heavy flours are used, add one cupful of gluten flour.

Roman Meal has found recent favor with many people. Here is my recipe for Roman Meal Muffins and Roman Meal Bread.

Roman Meal Muffins

2 cups unbleached white flour
2 cups Roman Meal
1-1/4 cups warm water
1 tablespoon active dry yeast, or 1 yeast cake
  dissolved in water.

Mix the flour, meal, and water. Add yeast and stir. Knead and let rise for 1 hour. Knead again and cut in sizes for muffins. Bake for 25 minutes at 400 degrees.

Roman Meal Bread

4 cups whole wheat flour
3 cups Roman Meal
1 cup gluten flour

Mix well.

3 cups warm water
1 tablespoon sweet butter
2 tablespoons active dry yeast

Knead twice. Bake at 350 degrees for 70 minutes.

Heart Cookies

3/4 cup raw sugar, firmly packed
1 cup unsalted butter
1/2 teaspoon sea salt
1 teaspoon vanilla extract
1 teaspoon almond extract
1-3/4 cups health food flour
1/2 cup wheat germ

Cream together raw sugar, butter, sea salt, vanilla, and almond extract. Add flour and wheat germ and mix well. Pinch off small pieces of dough and shape into hearts and place on ungreased cookie sheet. Bake for 15 minutes in 350 degree oven. Cool a few minutes before removing from cookie sheet to rack.

This recipe makes 5 dozen cookies.

To eat with the cookies, here is an easy recipe for ice cream.

Ice Cream

1 pint raw cream
1 tablespoon raw sugar
Add sugar to cream and whip contents

Place on top of bowls of Babcock peaches, blueberries, and pears and freeze.

A simple dinner for four can be prepared in a single pot —
a pressure cooker. I prefer the pressure cooker because the
speed with which it cooks preserves more of the flavor and
basic food value than does ordinary open-pot cooking.

Basic Beef Stew

1 pound stewing beef, cut into 1-inch cubes
1 yellow onion, quartered
2 fresh tomatoes
5 small red potatoes
1 package frozen string beans
1 package frozen Italian green beans
4 large or 6 small zucchini squash,
   cut into small pieces
4 medium-sized carrots, cut into 2-inch pieces
1 tablespoon salad herbs
2 tablespoons prepared low-salt bouillon
1 small can tomato sauce
1 cup distilled water

Place all ingredients in large pressure cooker. Cook over
medium flame. When pressure cooker begins to steam fully,
turn burner down and time for 25 minutes. Serve with
simple green salad.

Super Eggplant Casserole

1 eggplant
8 zucchini squash
4 ripe tomatoes
1 yellow onion
1/2 pound fresh string beans (or 1 cup frozen green
    beans as a substitute)
2 teaspoons unsalted butter
1/2 teaspoon garlic powder
8 slices raw cheddar cheese
    parmesan cheese
    salad herbs
6 bay leaves

First slice the eggplant in 1/4 inch wedges; slice the zucchini squash down the middle; and prepare fresh string beans whole. Place the three vegetables in a sauce pan, cover with water and parboil for about ten minutes.

Next, while vegetables are cooking, cut tomatoes and yellow onion in slices.

After vegetables are parboiled, place them in a shallow baking pan and distribute them evenly.

Place the sliced tomatoes, onions and raw cheddar cheese on top of the parboiled vegetables; sprinkle 1/2 teaspoons garlic powder on top, followed by a sprinkling of salad herbs; place bay leaves on top, then finish with a light sprinkling of parmesan cheese.

Place casserole in oven and bake for thirty-five minutes. Cheese should be completely melted before casserole is removed from the oven. Serve with a simple salad.

This recipe serves eight people. If frozen green beans are used, cook them first, separately from the other vegetables, in accordance with the package directions. Then add to the other casserole vegetables.

Here is a recipe for a simple salad.

Simple Salad

1 medium head Romaine lettuce
1 head Butter lettuce
1 peeled cucumber
6 stalks celery
salad dressing

Separate Romaine lettuce leaves and Butter lettuce leaves, wash carefully, blot dry with paper towel and place lettuce in a chilled salad bowl.

Slice cucumber and celery stalks in thin strips and place on top of lettuce.

Add salad dressing.

Simple Salad Dressing

1/4 cup apricot oil (or olive oil)
1/4 cup apple cider vinegar
    juice from one lemon
1/2 teaspoon salad herbs

Mix the above ingredients in a small jar, shake well and then mix with one or two tablespoons on the simple salad.

Baked Chicken Breasts

12 pieces chicken breast
1/2 cup distilled water
Garlic powder (not garlic salt)
Unsalted butter
Paprika

Preheat oven to broil. Lay chicken breasts bony side down in a flat baking pan. Dot each piece with unsalted butter on the top, then sprinkle garlic powder lightly on top, followed by a liberal sprinkling of paprika. Place chicken-filled flat pan under the broiler and brown both sides. This takes about 10 minutes. Remove pan from broiler and pour one-half cup of distilled water into bottom of pan. Place pan in oven, turn heat to 450 degrees and cook for 50-60 minutes (allow more time for larger chicken breasts).

For those individuals who enjoy trying something new, here is a recipe for Farina Dumplings.

Farina Dumplings

1/3 cup cream of wheat
2 tablespoons water
1 egg

Beat egg in 2 tablespoons of water. Add the result to cream of wheat and stir. Let stand until it stiffens; then gently drop in boiling water and cook until done.

These dumplings are excellent with cooked vegetables.

For those who have a sweet tooth, here is a recipe for Marzipan Spread which I use on bread and muffins. It should, however, be eaten in small amounts.

Marzipan Spread

1 cup finely ground almonds
2 tablespoons black strap molasses
2 tablespoons clover honey
6 tablespoons apricot oil

Mix ingredients thoroughly and keep in refrigerator.

A LAST WORD   23

As a general rule it is best to eat sparingly and to train your children to appreciate simple, natural foods.

False appetites are usually ingrained in children early in life. Provide a child with the proper dietary principles and he'll have a much better chance throughout the years of avoiding needless diseases and impaired sexual health. Teach the child sexual health attitudes that are free of superstitution and ignorance.

I stress again that a child's sexual health begins in the womb of the mother. The mother has a direct influence on the health of her child.

A good doctor is both a teacher and a friend. One of my former teachers and a good friend, Dr. Martin Fischer, said in his book of aphorisms entitled *Fischerisms:* "The doctor must set the example for the community; he must command respect." He also said: "Principles are the important things; the more you have of them the more knowledge can you carry."

I have presented to you, in this book, practical principles of nutrition. Respect and love for your body is the key. Self-discipline and obedience to nutritional principles open the door to good health and good sexual health.

A renowned scientist and thinking man, Thomas A. Edison, said, "The doctor of the future will give no medicine, but will interest his patients in diet and in the cause and prevention of disease."

This is my philosophy and my way of life.

Dr. Bieler's Natural Way to Sexual Health

Composition for this book was 11 on 13 Journal Roman, typeset on an
   IBM MTSC system by Austerity Type, Torrance, California.
Chapter Heads and Part Titles are Melior .
The text paper is Hamilton's Pennbrooke Offset, white, 60 lb.
For the cover, Holliston Mills' Sturdetan (Hunter Green, Line Weave)
   was stamped in gold foil.
Printing and binding were by New World Book Manufacturing, Hallan-
   dale, Florida.
Design and production was by Alan Baughman, Torrance, California.

DISTILLED WATER
1/2 - DILUTED
ZUCHINI   STRING BEANS   PEAS?
           STR. B. CEL PAR. 140
ZABINE

SALT 58
P-220   BIELEL BR-TH   ZUCHINI
PAGE 37 URIC ACID   CEL-STRING B-PAR
P 212   POTATO'S QUARD BEET TOPS
P 110   ZUCHINI PARSLEY CELERY
         (SEE 140 STRING BEANS)

P 118   2 ST CEL PAR
         PROTEIN + CAL TABS

P 123   SUGAR STARCH

P 145   PROST + IMP.
163   DIET (WT LOSS)
165

HIGH ALKA RESTORE LIV + KID
CLEANSE BODY TOXIC URIL FACIAL
CONDITION + CURES ARTARITIS
188 DIET

21 205 - 218 OPTIMUM FOOD +
                        MINUS
QHAP 22 REC